Integrating Artificial Intelligence Technology into Language Teacher Education

This volume provides five exploratory studies on the constraints and affordances of artificial intelligence (AI), specifically examining ChatGPT's applications among preservice teachers preparing to teach multilingual learners. Through detailed analysis of classroom implementation, student perceptions, and pedagogical outcomes, this collection offers groundbreaking insights into how large language models can transform teacher preparation programs. Three studies present firsthand accounts of preservice teachers' experiences with ChatGPT, revealing a pragmatic orientation where adoption hinges on student motivation, accelerated English language development, and ease of use. The remaining two studies investigate ChatGPT-produced text as an instructional tool, highlighting its potential for fostering critical analysis while emphasizing the necessity of thoughtful integration through careful teacher planning.

This volume speaks directly to graduate students, teacher educators, educational technology specialists, TESOL professionals, and researchers in applied linguistics and AI ethics. It bridges multiple disciplines including educational technology, second language acquisition, teacher preparation, multilingual education, and artificial intelligence in education. The research presented in this volume contributes to ongoing conversations about technological innovation in classrooms, ethical considerations in AI implementation, and evolving best practices for preparing teachers to work effectively with multilingual populations in technology-enhanced learning environments.

The chapters in this book were originally published as a special issue of *Computers in the Schools*.

Rod Case is Associate Professor of Teaching English as a Second Language at the University of Nevada, Reno, USA. He is one of three recipients of the Northern Nevada English Learning Initiative (NNELI). Case teaches courses in second language acquisition and second language assessment. His research interests include various topics in applied linguistics and second language acquisition.

Leping Liu is Professor of Quantitative Methods and Learning Sciences at the University of Nevada, Reno, USA. She has more than 20 years of higher education for two universities in the USA. She has taught over 25 courses in instructional technology, instructional design, information technology in education, statistics, research design, and counseling technologies. Liu has published over 20 books and numerous refereed journal articles, book chapters, and conference articles. She also is research editor for *Computers in the Schools* and editor in chief of the *International Journal of Technology in Teaching and Learning*.

Joseph Mintz is Professor of Inclusive Education at UCL's Institute of Education with a diverse background spanning software development, primary teaching in London schools, and higher education. His research focuses on autism education, teacher education for inclusion, and educational technology for children with special needs. His work bridges psychological knowledge and classroom practice, while his recent projects investigate AI applications in educational settings.

Integrating Artificial Intelligence Technology into Language Teacher Education

Challenges, Potentials and Assumptions

Edited by

Rod Case, Leping Liu, and Joseph Mintz

Routledge
Taylor & Francis Group
LONDON AND NEW YORK

First published 2026
by Routledge
4 Park Square, Milton Park, Abingdon, Oxon, OX14 4RN

and by Routledge
605 Third Avenue, New York, NY 10158

Routledge is an imprint of the Taylor & Francis Group, an informa business

British Library Cataloguing-in-Publication Data
A catalogue record for this book is available from the British Library

ISBN13: 978-1-041-12087-2 (hbk)
ISBN13: 978-1-041-12088-9 (pbk)
ISBN13: 978-1-003-66292-1 (ebk)

DOI: 10.4324/9781003662921

Typeset in Minion Pro
by codeMantra

Publisher's Note
The publisher accepts responsibility for any inconsistencies that may have arisen during the conversion of this book from journal articles to book chapters, namely the inclusion of journal terminology.

Contents

Citation Information

The chapters in this book were originally published in *Computers in the Schools*, Volume 42, Issue 2 (2025). When citing this material, please use the original page numbering for each article, as follows:

Chapter 1
Integrating AI Technology into Language Teacher Education: Challenges, Potentials, and Assumptions
Rod Case, Leping Liu and Joseph Mintz
Computers in the Schools, Volume 42, Issue 2 (2025), pp. 93–99

Chapter 2
Unveiling the Drivers of AI Integration Among Language Teachers: Integrating UTAUT and AI-TPACK
Nguyen Hoang Mai Tram
Computers in the Schools, Volume 42, Issue 2 (2025), pp. 100–120

Chapter 3
Assessing the Efficacy of Intelligent Tutoring Systems in Language Teacher Education: A Quantitative Study
Soumya Sankar Ghosh
Computers in the Schools, Volume 42, Issue 2 (2025), pp. 121–144

Chapter 4
The Integration of ChatGPT in English for Foreign Language Course: Elevating AI Writing Assistant Acceptance
Urai Salam
Computers in the Schools, Volume 42, Issue 2 (2025), pp. 145–165

Chapter 5
Assessing AI and Human Writing Skills: A Comparative Analysis of Pre-Service Teachers' Perceptions
Maria Navío-Inglés, Sergio Tirado-Olivares, Javier del Olmo-Muñoz and Jesús Guzmán Mora
Computers in the Schools, Volume 42, Issue 2 (2025), pp. 166–186

Chapter 6

ChatGPT-Produced Content as a Resource in the Language Education Classroom: A Guiding Hand
Rod E. Case and Leping Liu
Computers in the Schools, Volume 42, Issue 2 (2025), pp. 187–211

Notes on Contributors

Rod Case, College of Education and Human Development, University of Nevada, Reno, USA.

Leping Liu, College of Education and Human Development, University of Nevada, Reno, USA.

Joseph Mintz, UCL Institute of Education, University College London, UK.

Jesús Guzmán Mora, University of Castilla-La Mancha, Albacete, Spain.

Maria Navío-Inglés, University of Castilla-La Mancha, Albacete, Spain.

Javier del Olmo-Muñoz, University of Castilla-La Mancha, Albacete, Spain.

Urai Salam, Universitas Tanjungpura Pontianak, Indonesia.

Soumya Sankar Ghosh, VIT Bhopal University, India.

Sergio Tirado-Olivares, University of Castilla-La Mancha, Albacete, Spain.

Nguyen Hoang Mai Tram, Ho Chi Minh City University of Foreign Languages - Information Technology, Vietnam.

Preface

Rod Case, Leping Liu and Joseph Mintz

Although the use of Artificial Intelligence (AI) in the classroom is not new to Language Teacher Education (LTE)—computer-assisted language learning has been a mainstay in LTE for decades—the introduction of ChatGPT represents a shift in how it might be used in the classroom. Prior to ChatGPT, AI relied on pattern matching and keyword usage to formulate responses. Programs were capable of simple vocabulary games and quizzes, scripted dialogues, and pronunciation drills. Responses were limited to predetermined phrases and could not approximate human speech. ChatGPT was different, relying instead on large language models to learn from interactions and adapt its responses. Gone were the awkward, scripted dialogues. ChatGPT could engage advanced students in sophisticated exchanges on any number of topics, adjusting for communication breakdowns by modifying vocabulary level. Beginning students could study vocabulary lists and, if needed, query ChatGPT in their home language when they had questions.

The flexibility of ChatGPT opened the door to more authentic communicative practice. Teachers could now design tasks that emulated real-world discourse—conversation, debate, or role-playing. However, given the time commitment involved in testing the effectiveness of classroom-based applications of ChatGPT via longitudinal studies across varied settings, early research focused on understanding the subjective experiences and practical concerns of preservice teachers (PSTs). Accordingly, research centered on gauging the extent to which PSTs' perceptions of and experiences with ChatGPT predicted its use in the classroom. While researchers were often optimistic, PSTs remained skeptical. Their concerns included limited professional development, untested impacts on student learning, and doubts about the trustworthiness of AI-generated content. Predictors for adoption included previous personal use of ChatGPT, institutional support or mentorship, and concerns about data privacy and ethics.

Perceptions of teacher learning provided a building block for researchers to explore how ChatGPT might act as a mediator for learning. While frameworks guiding its use exist, few universities have established official policies. In fact, a U.S.-wide poll conducted in 2024 by *Inside Higher Education* found that just 20% of 331 surveyed colleges had policies concerning AI-based technology. Although 78% had offered training, only 14% had reviewed policies regarding student preparedness for AI use in the workplace.

Findings showed sharp differences in how disciplines have approached AI—differences rooted both in epistemological orientations and in disciplinary priorities. The arts and humanities tend to focus on interpretation, subjectivity, and the expression of a unique vision across changing contexts. For example, the National Endowment for the Humanities currently funds grants that explore public understanding of ethics and AI; the connections between data science, art, narrative, and public policy; and the role of AI in scholarly rigor. STEM disciplines, in contrast, seek objectivity and rely on the scientific method to verify knowledge. AI use in STEM is deeply embedded and valued for its ability to increase productivity—provided it yields accurate and reliable analysis.

As language teacher educators, we often describe ourselves as researcher-practitioners—living between the hyphen. As researchers—typically located neither within STEM nor the humanities—we publish in educational journals that require human subjects' protection, evidence-based analysis, and adherence to academic integrity in authorship. Through this kind of scholarship, we aim to model integrity, intellectual curiosity, and a vision of the teacher as a life-long learner. We hope our students will share their expertise, collaborate with peers, and see professional development as both a vocation and an extension of their evolving identity.

A ChatGPT for this side of the hyphen would speak with the sociological voice that many humanities scholars bring to their work. It would recognize that language learning is mediated by social interaction and shaped by contextual variables such as identity, motivation, and perception. At the same time, it would balance this contextualized view with insights from the cognitive linguistic tradition, drawing on scholars such as Robin Lakoff, Mark Johnson, and Leonard Talmy—those who resisted explaining language as modular or autonomous and advocating instead for an embodied view of language.

On the other side of the hyphen—as practitioners—our work is grounded in the classroom, the world we prepare our students to enter. That classroom is not a small place. For the TESOL educator, it spans the globe. England began spreading the English language nearly 300 years ago—think, for instance, of Defoe's *Robinson Crusoe* and the British literary tradition. Today, there are more English speakers living in countries where English is not the medium of instruction than in those where it is. With its focus on identity and the ways speakers leverage multiple languages to create meaning, translanguaging—sometimes referred to as code-switching—emerges as a framework to account for the ever-expanding circle of English speakers and the multiplicity of identities they bring to language learning.

Technology figures prominently in this shift. Chatbots and AI-powered platforms give learners opportunities to use English for self-defined purposes. Programs like Duolingo and Rosetta Stone, though sometimes critiqued for their decontextualized or outdated "code-based" views of language, should not be dismissed. Such programs provide access to the building blocks of language. Modern technology affords students the opportunity to use them at home, preparing them for the kinds of contextualized language instruction contemporary language teachers are capable of delivering.

While recent AI developments have introduced content-specific bots, there is still work to be done. Chatbots like Merlyn Mind, Diffit, and Eduaide are tailored for familiar classroom tasks—lesson planning, assessment creation, and activity generation. Yet they are not true conversational partners for teacher educators who live between the hyphens. Rather, they function as efficiency tools with interactive features.

The research presented in this book is one step toward redefining that conversation. It brings together scholars from around the world to explore the intersection of language learning, teaching, and AI. Its audience is teacher educators and researchers interested in teacher education who prepare PSTs to work with multilingual learners. Five chapters present findings on how teacher educators have engaged PSTs with ChatGPT—sending them into classrooms and encouraging reflection on language use and learning from both sides of the hyphen.

Integrating AI Technology into Language Teacher Education: Challenges, Potentials, and Assumptions

The emergence of ChatGPT, a chatbot powered by artificial intelligence (AI), has transformed language education and captured the attention of the public and educators alike. ChatGPT draws on large-scale language models (LLMs), allowing it to emulate human language, decision-making, and planning while interacting with users (Lee et al., 2020). Its use of LLMs distinguishes it from previous chatbots, which relied exclusively on keywords, pattern matching, and user input to form responses, making it a powerful tool for teachers who need assistance with creating classroom exercises, worksheets, and assessments.

Research in this field initially began with explorations of the perceptions of pre-service teachers (PSTs) about ChatGPT, emphasizing how classroom practice was shaped by PSTs' perceptions and knowledge of ChatGPT (e.g., Javier & Moorhouse, 2024; Jeon, 2024; Jeon & Lee, 2023). This research showed that PSTs often question the tradeoffs ChatGPT presents. As an instructional tool, on the surface, ChatGPT-created instruction seems to check all the boxes, providing rapidly produced lessons and classroom exercises, AI-powered individualized language instruction, and a "human-like" intellect capable of effortlessly producing cogent analyses of complex educational questions (Cooper, 2023; Farrokhnia et al., 2024; Skrabut, 2023). However, the technical wizardry that allows ChatGPT to effortlessly create lessons is out of sync with the vision that PSTs hold of instruction. In other words, the use of AI-generated instruction needs to be informed by their still-emerging pedagogical voice as PSTs.

The research field as a whole, and what it revealed about the thoughts of PSTs, gestures toward a larger point: we should push the research agenda in language teacher education (LTE) beyond the argument that teaching is just a technical exercise in efficiently and quickly producing classroom exercises. For us, it is also a personal endeavor. Such research into the use of GPT in the classroom should encompass the excluded voices, thoughts, emotions, experiences, and feelings of PSTs themselves.

Teacher educators in LTE and other teacher education sub-disciplines interested in examining the use of ChatGPT now face the same question: how to make use of it in authentic ways that will contribute to learning. They all bring a type of bespoke model of instruction to their individual practice, shaped by the diverse linguistic, cultural, and academic experiences they bring to that practice. Utilizing ChatGPT to create or design instruction does offer a means of rapidly creating coursework, exams, and analyses of pedagogical content that expand in their abilities with each new iteration. As such, its introduction places a responsibility on researchers to balance the seemingly limitless technical potential of ChatGPT against the pedagogical voice teachers and teacher educators bring to their own instruction.

This special issue is a call to examine the interplay between the perceptions and knowledge of ChatGPT that PSTs bring to the language classroom and how teacher educators can navigate the two in the courses they design. Before summarizing those contributions, however, an overview of the assumptions about learning and teaching with ChatGPT is in order. The three assumptions below are taken from the still-developing research in LTE and ChatGPT and are meant as a brief framework on current trends driving the use of ChatGPT in LTE.

Assumptions in the use of AI in language teacher education

The studies in this special issue, while varied in their methodologies and underlying beliefs about second language development, share a number of assumptions about the affordances that the use of AI-based technology provides language teachers and language learners. We list below our view of the three most significant:

1. *AI-based technology can reduce teacher workload* by assisting them with developing lessons (Farrokhnia et al., 2024; Skrabut, 2023), worksheets, and assessments (Kohnke, 2023). However, the use of AI-based technology, ChatGPT in particular, requires close oversight by the teacher (Li et al., 2024) that reflects students' needs. Lessons written by ChatGPT have to be reviewed; test content has to account for the depth of the students' current understanding; and feedback given on assignments also has to reflect an understanding of students' individual needs. ChatGPT's ability to relieve teachers of this responsibility is laudable, but it also raises questions about how teachers will leverage ChatGPT's time-saving benefits without sacrificing their pedagogical voice. For instance, how will professional knowledge and classroom experience shape or be shaped by ChatGPT when it is filtered through a large language learning model like ChatGPT? Additionally, how can preservice teachers assess ChatGPT's decision-making processes as they develop their pedagogical voices?
2. *Technology provides a means of engaging students* in opportunities to learn language through practice with LLMs. The research on this informs teachers as to how ChatGPT can assist in everyday instructional tasks while recognizing the larger functions of attitudinal and emotional factors that accompany instruction. Regarding the former, ChatGPT can provide effective individualized tutoring, which can offer targeted feedback to learners in terms of pronunciation and speaking (Jia et al., 2022) and grammar (Al-Abdullatif & Alsubaie, 2022). Specific to research in this journal, ChatGPT also shows promise in building composition skills across a variety of genres (Kohnke, 2023; Kohnke et al., 2023) as well as connected proficiency in specific subskills such as grammar and vocabulary. While some research indicates that students tend to lose motivation after interacting with the same program repeatedly (Chen et al., 2016), this is the result of an overreliance on these technologies. A stronger case can be made for their potential to build motivation by selectively providing practice targeted to the students' learning levels (Yildiz Durak, 2023). Such judicious attention to the use of AI-powered bots has been shown to build confidence across a number of language-related tasks (Chang et al., 2022).
3. *If AI-based technology is capable of producing content that is accurate and appropriate for language learning*, it has the potential to serve as a scaffold to enhance learning. While there are a number of studies that have explored the accuracy

of ChatGPT-produced text in diverse fields (Gilson et al., 2022; Huh, 2023; Katz et al., 2023; Yeadon et al., 2023); and its prowess as a "writer" (Elkins & Chun, 2020), these have most often been set within the larger discussion of the potential for plagiarism. While there is an emerging body of research examining AI in teacher education, the few studies that have examined the extent to which ChatGPT-produced text can serve as a scaffold for learning among pre-service or in-service teachers in LTE have been promising. Li et al. (2024), for instance, found that pre-service teachers who had the opportunity to interact with ChatGPT to complete their assignments demonstrated higher levels of critical thinking than their peers. Li et al.'s (2024) explanation was that their awareness of ChatGPT's potential to produce inaccurate responses caused them to check their own work against outside sources more carefully.

Collectively, the assumptions described above suggest that LLMs like ChatGPT open possibilities for teachers to reduce their workload and provide individualized instruction to students. However, these are not without their tradeoffs. The net effect of using ChatGPT may not be a straightforward reduction in the teacher's workload but rather a shift in responsibility that still requires time and calls for them to find ways to negotiate how they will draw on the affordances of ChatGPT and perhaps redefine their pedagogical voice. With respect to teachers' motivations and perceptions of technology, it seems clear that the use of ChatGPT is predicated upon its utility and efficacy in terms of its holistic impact on teaching and learning. This research, however, has to be considered in light of the dynamic nature of AI technology. ChatGPT 4.0, for instance, has, at time of writing, just been recently released. It represents a significant improvement over its predecessors, allowing users to program customized AI-powered bots. The technology continues to develop rapidly, with new innovations being released almost every month. Even now, with very little formal training, any teacher can customize a special tutorial to support a class of language learners or even a single student. This represents a level of technological flexibility which has the potential to redefine language teacher education. Future research will need to keep pace with these changes, providing detailed examinations into the intersection between perception and instructional practice. One of the challenges both for K-12 educators and for the educational research community in general is keeping pace with the development of these innovations in the commercial technology industry. Although it is hard right now to be sure how best to address this disjuncture in the speed at which research occurs compared to commercial technology developments, we will need to somehow keep up with these changes, and maintain a focus on pedagogical instruction, learning, and the role of the teacher, including the pre-service teacher. This is particularly difficult for teacher educators who need to somehow "guess" the future in preparing their students for the world of the classroom.

The five manuscripts included in this special edition represent a staging post in the journey to take on this call for research in this rapidly developing arena. Three offer accounts of PSTs' perceptions of using ChatGPT. The fourth and fifth examine the use of ChatGPT-produced text with PSTs. A summary and guiding narrative of the five manuscripts follows.

The manuscripts

The five research areas which the manuscripts present were not meant to be exclusive. Rather, they represent a guide, a starting point for researchers to describe the ways in which language teacher education is informed by the social and cultural practices of the language learners in their respective communities. The broadest of the manuscripts, the first in the collection, by Tram, examined the attitudinal determinants of experienced and inexperienced teachers in adopting or not adopting AI chatbots in Vietnam. This study combined two measures of attitudinal determinants, the Unified Theory of Acceptance and Use of Technology (UTAUT) and the Technological Pedagogical Content Knowledge (TPACK) framework. Tram's findings demonstrated that teachers who viewed chatbots as a tool that could motivate their students and enhance learning would adopt the use of chatbots if it was possible to learn how to use the chatbot rapidly.

The second paper, by Ghosh, examines the influence of Intelligent Tutoring Systems (ITS) in the teacher education classroom in India. While Ghosh shared many of the same questions with the first paper, Ghosh drew from a broader corpus of data including student work, test scores, and observations and, of course, examined the use of ITS. Findings link teachers' adoption of ITS to its ease of use, efficacy in promoting language learning, and usefulness in the classroom. Complementary work in the third paper in the collection, by Salam, turned to an investigation of language learners' perceptions of ChatGPT in Indonesia. Mirroring the sentiments of the teachers in both Tram and Ghosh, Salam found that language learners were more likely to accept the use of ChatGPT based upon its usefulness.

The remaining manuscripts analyzed the potential of ChatGPT-produced text itself as a resource for learning. The fourth contribution, Navío-Inglés and colleagues' mixed-methods study of 154 PSTs in Spain, investigated PSTs' attitudes about ChatGPT-produced texts. ChatGPT-produced texts were rated significantly higher on text structure and organization, while human-produced texts conveyed more emotion. The findings are an important step forward in understanding the different rhetorical patterning endemic to ChatGPT- versus human-produced text and build upon assumption three above.

In the final paper, in an investigation of PSTs' appraisals of ChatGPT-produced texts in the US, and the potential of ChatGPT-produced text to enhance understanding of pedagogy, Case and Liu similarly build upon assumption three. Case and Liu set their work within an online teacher education pre-service course in multilingual teaching methods and examined PSTs' appraisals of ChatGPT- and human-produced work. The findings demonstrated that PSTs' appraisals were more favorable of ChatGPT content than human-produced content, and these appraisals were also conditioned by where ChatGPT was introduced into the assignment and if the prompts for ChatGPT were produced by the students or the instructor. Instructor-produced prompts were appraised more favorably than those produced by students, as was the positioning of ChatGPT-produced text at the beginning and the middle of the task versus the end of the task.

What is next for AI-based language learning and teaching is a search for how to define teacher-directed use of ChatGPT. Early research into teachers' perceptions of using ChatGPT and AI in the classroom provided valuable insights into initial teachers' concerns, including efficacy, usefulness, and the learning curve associated with using ChatGPT and other AI-based chatbots. Research into PSTs' use of ChatGPT and other AI chatbots in the classroom has shown that ChatGPT offered a viable tool for creating content that PSTs appraised favorably. However, these findings have also opened larger questions about how teachers can leverage the technical affordances of ChatGPT as a tutor and an aid in developing class content while maintaining their pedagogical voice. Building on this research, this is a call for a second generation of research into how these questions can be addressed with LLMs such as ChatGPT. Researchers can explore how the pedagogical voice is shaped across the different contexts in which language education takes place while maintaining an eye on constant advances. Research into how AI chatbots might complement or interrupt the pedagogical voice is one avenue of exploration. Research can also expand our understanding of the choices teachers make about using AI bots and how those choices vary with students' expectations, age, and proficiency. As noted, the advances of the technology industry are rapid, and such rapidity often precludes the possibility of proper consideration of the impact of such technology on education, whether positive or negative (Mintz et al., 2023). In respect of language teacher education and AI&ED, the international research community has an important role to play, in creating a space for reflection, thinking, due consideration of varying perspectives, and of course giving primacy to the role of evidence.

Disclosure statement

No potential conflict of interest was reported by the author(s).

References

Al-Abdullatif, A. M., & Alsubaie, M. A. (2022). Using digital learning platforms for teaching Arabic literacy: A post-pandemic mobile learning scenario in Saudi Arabia. *Sustainability*, *14*(19), 11868. https://doi.org/10.3390/su141911868

Chang, C.-Y., Hwang, G.-J., & Gau, M.-L. (2022). Promoting students' learning achievement and self-efficacy: A mobile chatbot approach for nursing training. *British Journal of Educational Technology*, *53*(1), 171–188. https://doi.org/10.1111/bjet.13158

Chen, J. A., Tutwiler, M. S., Metcalf, S. J., Kamarainen, A., Grotzer, T., & Dede, C. (2016). A multi-user virtual environment to support students' self-efficacy and interest in science: A latent growth model analysis. *Learning and Instruction*, *41*, 11–22. https://doi.org/10.1016/j.learninstruc.2015.09.007

Cooper, G. (2023). Examining science education in ChatGPT: An exploratory study of generative artificial intelligence. *Journal of Science Education and Technology*, *32*(3), 444–452. https://doi.org/10.1007/s10956-023-10039-y

Elkins, K., & Chun, J. (2020). Can GPT-3 pass a writer's Turing test? *Journal of Cultural Analytics*, *5*(2), 1–6. https://doi.org/10.22148/001c.17212

Farrokhnia, M., Banihashem, S. K., Noroozi, O., & Wals, A. (2024). A SWOT analysis of ChatGPT: Implications for educational practice and research. *Innovations in Education and Teaching International*, *61*(3), 460–474. https://doi.org/10.1080/14703297.2023.2195846

Gilson, A., Safranek, C., Huang, T., Socrates, V., Chi, L., Taylor, R. A., & Chartash, D. (2022). How does ChatGPT perform on the medical licensing exams? The implications of large language models for medical education and knowledge assessment. *bioRxiv*. 2022.12.23.22283901; https://doi.org/10.1101/2022.12.23.22283901

Javier, D. R., & Moorhouse, B. L. (2024). Developing secondary school English language learners' productive and critical use of ChatGPT. *TESOL Journal*, *15*(2), 755–756. https://doi.org/10.1002/tesj.755

Huh, S. (2023). Are ChatGPT's knowledge and interpretation ability comparable to those of medical students in Korea for taking a parasitology examination? *Journal of Educational Evaluation for Health Professions*, *20*(, 1. https://doi.org/10.3352/jeehp.2023.20.1

Jeon, J. (2024). Exploring AI chatbot affordances in the EFL classroom: Young learners' experiences and perspectives. *Computer Assisted Language Learning*, *37*(1-2), 1–26. https://doi.org/10.1080/09588221.2021.2021241

Jeon, J., & Lee, S. (2023). Large language models in education: A focus on the complementary relationship between human teachers and ChatGPT. *Education and Information Technologies*, *28*(12), 15873–15892. https://doi.org/10.1007/s10639-023-11834-1

Katz, D. M., Bommarito, M. J., Gao, S., & Arredondo, P. (2023). GPT-4 passes the bar exam. Philisophical Transactions of the Royal Society. A 382, 20230254. https://doi.org/10.1098/rsta.2023.0254

Kohnke, L. (2023). A pedagogical chatbot: A supplemental language learning tool. *RELC Journal*, *54*(3), 828–838. https://doi.org/10.1177/00336882211067054

Kohnke, L., Moorhouse, B. L., & Zou, D. (2023). ChatGPT for language teaching and learning. *RELC Journal*, *54*(2), 537–550. https://doi.org/10.1177/00336882231162868

Lee, J. H., Yang, H., Shin, D., & Kim, H. (2020). Chatbots. *ELT Journal*, *74*(3), 338–344. https://doi.org/10.1093/elt/ccaa03

Li, T., Ji, Y., & Zhan, Z. (2024). Expert or machine? Comparing the effect of pairing student teacher with in-service teacher and CHATGPT on their critical thinking, learning performance, and cognitive load in an integrated-stem course. *Asia Pacific Journal of Education*, *44*(1), 45–60. https://doi.org/10.1080/02188791.2024.2305163

Mintz, J., Holmes, W., Liu, L., & Perez-Ortiz, M. (2023). Artificial Intelligence and K-12 education: Possibilities, pedagogies and risks. *Computers in the Schools*, *40*(4), 325–333. https://doi.org/10.1080/07380569.2023.2279870

Skrabut, S. (2023). 80 ways to use ChatGPT in the classroom: Using AI to enhance teaching and learning. *Independent*.

Yeadon, W., Inyang, O.-O., Mizouri, A., Peach, A., & Testrow, C. P. (2023). The death of the short-form physics essay in the coming AI revolution. *Physics Education*, *58*(3), 035027. https://doi.org/10.1088/1361-6552/acc5cf

Yildiz Durak, Y. H. (2023). Conversational agent-based guidance: Examining the effect of chatbot usage frequency and satisfaction on visual design self-efficacy, engagement, satisfaction, and learner autonomy. *Education and Information Technologies*, *28*(1), 471–488. https://doi.org/10.1007/s10639-022-11149-7

Rod Case and Leping Liu

Joseph Mintz

Unveiling the Drivers of AI Integration Among Language Teachers: Integrating UTAUT and AI-TPACK

Nguyen Hoang Mai Tram

ABSTRACT

Artificial intelligence (AI) offers numerous benefits to the field of language education, making it crucial to understand the factors influencing language teachers' adoption of these technologies. This study investigates the determinants of language teachers' adoption of AI chatbots in educational settings. Drawing on the Unified Theory of Acceptance and Use of Technology (UTAUT) and the Technological Pedagogical Content Knowledge (TPACK) framework, a comprehensive model of AI adoption among language teachers is proposed and tested. Data were collected from 276 language teachers in Vietnam through an online survey. Partial Least Square-Structural Equation Modeling (PLS-SEM) was employed to analyze the data. Results indicate that AI adoption intent significantly predicts AI integration, while performance expectancy, effort expectancy, and AI self-efficacy are key determinants of AI adoption intent. AI-TPACK emerges as a crucial factor, strongly influencing AI self-efficacy, performance expectancy, and effort expectancy. Facilitation is found to be a significant predictor of AI-TPACK. These findings enhance the theoretical framework of AI adoption in language education and provide valuable insights for fostering effective AI integration among language teachers.

Introduction

Teachers increasingly use artificial intelligence (AI) in their teaching, thanks to the significant benefits this technology brings to both teaching and learning processes. In the domain of language education, numerous studies have indicated that integrating AI into teaching activities enhances student engagement, facilitates personalized learning, improves language proficiency, and increases overall learner satisfaction (Kohnke et al., 2023; Yang & Li, 2024). Specifically, for language teachers, AI serves as a valuable tool in creating lesson plans, suggesting relevant exercises, finding suitable teaching materials, and supporting professional development (Tram & Tran-Thanh, 2024). This contributes to saving time and enhancing teaching effectiveness. However, the successful integration of AI into teaching practices heavily depends upon the teachers' ability and manner of usage (Teo, 2011). Advanced technological tools, regardless of their sophistication, will fail to achieve their full potential if not employed effectively within each teacher's specific teaching methodology (Teo, 2011). Thus, the role of the teacher extends beyond mere technology adoption; it requires an understanding of how to optimize AI to meet specific teaching needs and objectives (An et al., 2023).

Vietnam has emerged as a dynamic player in the global push for digital transformation, particularly in education. The government has prioritized digital transformation as a key driver of educational reform, as highlighted in the National Digital Transformation Strategy to 2030. Despite this, the extent to which language teachers are utilizing AI chatbots remains largely unexplored. By focusing on Vietnam, this study sheds light on how government initiatives intersect with individual teacher practices, providing a nuanced understanding of AI adoption in a rapidly evolving educational landscape. In addition, most research on AI in education focuses on the technical aspects, such as system development (Divekar et al., 2022), while the factors influencing teachers' acceptance and use of AI in language teaching receive far less attention. In addition, research on language teachers' perceptions of AI is still in its early stages (e.g., An et al., 2023; Mohamed, 2024), while AI tools are developing rapidly and continuously. Therefore, there is a need for more in-depth studies to understand the relationship between language teachers and AI tools. Addressing these gaps is critical, as teacher acceptance and sustained use of AI are prerequisites for achieving benefits of technology integration (Tram & Tran-Thanh, 2024). The current study aims to fill these gaps by examining the factors influencing language teachers' use of AI. Insights from this research will provide a foundation for guiding policies and strategies that promote the sustainable and effective integration of AI in language teaching.

The current study employs the Unified Theory of Acceptance and Use of Technology (UTAUT) in conjunction with the Technological Pedagogical Content Knowledge (TPACK) framework to investigate the determinants of teachers' AI usage behavior. UTAUT has been widely applied to explore how individuals' perceptions of technology influence their behavioral intentions regarding technology adoption (Venkatesh et al., 2003). Meanwhile, TPACK offers a framework for evaluating teachers' knowledge concerning the integration of technology, content, and pedagogy (Mishra & Koehler, 2006), which is considered a crucial extension to UTAUT (An et al., 2023). Previous studies, such as Teo et al. (2019), have effectively combined

UTAUT and TPACK to predict teachers' intentions to utilize Web 2.0 technologies in educational settings. The integration of these two models has shown significant predictive power concerning teachers' intentions to adopt new technologies. Building on the UTAUT and TPACK frameworks, this study investigates the factors predicting language teachers' integration of AI into their teaching practices, leading to the following research question: What are the key antecedents influencing language teachers' adoption of AI?

Literature review

AI chatbots in language education

AI chatbots are computer programs that simulate human conversations through audio or text forms, serving as virtual assistants to users. Existing literature has shown that the utilization of AI chatbots in language education presents numerous benefits for language teachers (Kohnke et al., 2023). For instance, Tram and Tran-Thanh (2024) suggested that AI chatbots such as ChatGPT, Bard, Bing can assist EFL teachers with various tasks such as generating lesson plans, creating exercises, finding teaching materials, professional development. In the classroom, teachers can support students by helping them utilize AI chatbots to look up vocabulary, find example sentences, translate, and learn particular grammar concepts (Kohnke et al., 2023). Additionally, AI chatbots provide a consistent and unbiased assessment of student performance, which can help teachers identify learning gaps and tailor their instruction accordingly (Lo, 2023). For professional growth, ChatGPT can assist educators by providing resources and insights into new teaching strategies, technologies, and materials (Rudolph et al., 2023). This helps educators keep up with the latest developments and techniques in education, ultimately improving their teaching effectiveness. AI chatbots' versatility in offering personalized learning experiences, automated assessment and feedback, virtual assistance, content creation, and various other educational applications underscores their significance in modern language education settings.

UTAUT model

The Unified Theory of Acceptance and Use of Technology (UTAUT) is a comprehensive model that investigate the acceptance of a system or technology (Venkatesh et al., 2003). The UTAUT has been extensively employed by researchers to elucidate the acceptance of technological innovations, particularly within various educational contexts (Xiaohong et al., 2024). For instance, UTAUT has been applied in investigating mobile learning acceptance (Fagan, 2019), students' use of learning management systems

(Raza et al., 2021), social-media-based learning (Rahman et al., 2021). Additionally, the UTAUT model is also applied to many of the latest educational technologies, including augmented reality acceptance among university students (Ustun et al., 2024), virtual reality classroom (Ogegbo et al., 2024), metaverse integrated learning environments (Wiangkham & Vongvit, 2024), teachers' and students' acceptance and use of generative artificial intelligence (Xiaohong et al., 2024) such as ChatGPT (Budhathoki et al., 2024), AI-based assessment systems (Shahid et al., 2024), and academic advising chatbot (Bilquise et al., 2024).

In the field of language education, UTAUT has been extended and modified to explore teachers' and learners' acceptance and use of technologies. For instance, motivation has been added to the UTAUT framework to explain EFL learners' acceptance of LMOOCs (Hsu, 2023) and undergraduate EFL learners' intention to use ChatGPT for English learning (Xu & Thien, 2024). While many studies focus on the antecedents of technology adoption, Zou et al. (2022) emphasize consequential factors such as students' satisfaction and perceived learning performance when integrating smartphones in EFL classrooms. When researching EFL teachers' acceptance, the Technological Pedagogical Content Knowledge (TPACK) framework is incorporated into the UTAUT model to understand their intention to use technology (An et al., 2023). Some studies, such as those by Shen et al. (2023) and Li et al. (2020), have indicated that facilitating conditions are the most significant predictor of behavioral intention to adopt smartphones for informal language learning. In contrast, other studies have suggested that effort expectancy and performance expectancy are more important than facilitating conditions in predicting behavioral intentions to use technology among EFL learners and teachers (Ahmed et al., 2024; Chun &Yunus, 2023). The UTAUT model is a crucial framework for deploying new technologies, clarifying factors affecting user acceptance, and suggesting ways to increase adoption rates. Understanding and applying these factors improves technology integration and enhances the learning experience for both teachers and students.

TPACK

Technological Pedagogical Content Knowledge (TPACK), introduced by Mishra and Koehler (2006), provides a framework for effective technology integration in teaching. Emphasizing the intersection of technology, pedagogy, and content knowledge, TPACK identifies seven components: technological knowledge (TK), pedagogical knowledge (PK), content knowledge (CK), pedagogical content knowledge (PCK), technological pedagogical knowledge (TPK), technological content knowledge (TCK), and technological pedagogical content knowledge (TPACK). This framework is crucial for predicting the successful implementation of technology in various educational settings. For example, it has been applied to pre-service teachers' technology integration (Habibi et al., 2023), the intention to use technology among higher education teachers in emerging countries (Al-Adwan et al., 2024), the inclination of pre-service teachers to integrate AI into STEM education (Sun et al., 2024), the acceptance of virtual reality in science education by preservice teachers (Thohir et al., 2023), and the behavioral intention of English teachers to use artificial intelligence in middle schools (An et al., 2023). Although both UTAUT and TPACK have been independently utilized in research on technology acceptance, integrating these two theories is essential for understanding language teachers' AI integration. This study, by leveraging multiple theoretical perspectives, makes a novel contribution to identifying factors influencing language teachers' AI use, thereby informing policy and practice in the context of language education.

Hypothesis development

AI adoption intent and AI integration

Within the UTAUT, behavioral intention and usage behavior are two important resulting variables to explain technology acceptance (Venkatesh et al., 2003, 2012). Behavioral intention refers to how likely users are to adopt a technology, whereas usage behavior denotes the actual implementation of that technology (Davis, 1989). The theories of reasoned action (TRA) and planned behavior (TPB) have highlighted that intention is the strongest predictor of actual use behavior (Ajzen, 1991; Fishbein & Ajzen, 1975). In this study, AI adoption intent is termed as the extent to which language teachers are willing to use AI chatbots in the future (Choi et al., 2023). Meanwhile, AI integration is the habits, and action of users when interacting with AI, which is measured using language teachers' frequency of using AI chatbots (Nie et al., 2020). The strong association between AI adoption intent and AI integration is revealed in existing educational technology literature, such as students' use of AI-based voice assistants (Al Shamsi et al., 2022), students' adoption of AI-based teacher-bots for learning in higher education (Pillai et al., 2024), the use of ChatGPT in informal digital learning of English (Liu & Ma, 2024). Drawing on these insights, the present study examines the effect of language teachers' AI adoption intent on AI integration with the following hypothesis:

H1: AI adoption intent can positively predict AI integration.

Performance expectancy, effort expectancy, and AI adoption intent

Performance expectancy is defined as the degree to which individuals feel the adoption of the new technologies is beneficial to their task or work (Venkatesh et al., 2003). Performance expectancy has been shown to positively affect technology adoption in various educational contexts, such as mobile learning (Fagan, 2019), e-learning (Khan et al., 2023), AI-based applications (Choi et al., 2023; Pillai et al., 2024; Tram et al., 2024). In this study, performance expectancy is the extent to which language teachers believe that their job performance could be improved with the support of AI chatbots in teaching-related activities. Prior studies on AI technologies in education have indicated that performance expectancy motivate teachers to use and accept AI, such as teachers' acceptance of AI learning platform (Xiaohong et al., 2024), educators' use of AI in higher education (Jain & Raghuram, 2024), teachers' use of AI in middle schools (An et al., 2023), Indonesian pre-service teachers' adoption of virtual reality in science education (Thohir et al., 2023), Chinese preservice teachers' use of AI in STEM education (Sun et al., 2024). Based on previous research's findings, language teachers are more likely to use an AI chatbot if they perceive it to be useful in preparing lesson plans, creating tests, grading students, and other teaching-related tasks (Tram & Tran-Thanh, 2024). Accordingly, H2 is formulated:

H2: Performance expectancy can positively predict AI adoption intent.

Effort expectancy represents how easy it is to use a technology (Venkatesh et al., 2003). Hence, effort expectancy is similar to the perceived ease of use in Technology Acceptance Model (Davis, 1989), and ease of use in Diffusion of Innovation Theory (Venkatesh et al., 2003). Effort expectancy serve as a strong antecedent of behavioral intention in educational technology adoption, as supported by research on students' and teachers' acceptance of AI-based learning environments, such as AI voice assistants (Al Shamsi et al., 2022), academic advising chatbots (Bilquise et al., 2024), AI teacher-bots (Pillai et al., 2024), ChatGPT (Liu & Ma, 2024). In this study, effort expectancy is conceptualized as the degree to which language teachers perceive ChatGPT as having a user-friendly and straightforward interface, saving time and effort in teaching-related tasks. Effort expectancy has been shown to significantly affect teachers' AI adoption intent in previous studies on AI technologies in education (e.g., Choi et al., 2023; Sun et al., 2024; Thohir et al., 2023; Xiaohong et al., 2024). When an AI-driven chatbot is user-friendly and does not require effort, language teachers are more likely to use it to attain the expected performance. In light of this, the following hypothesis is posited:

H3: Effort expectancy can positively predict AI adoption intent.

AI self-efficacy and AI adoption intent

Grounded in the social cognitive theory (Bandura, 1986), self-efficacy is related to people's confidence in performing certain tasks rather than their actual skills. Self-efficacy is also a significant determiner of one's behavior. Aligning with this definition, computer self-efficacy represents an individual's belief or attitude regarding their ability to effectively use technology (Compeau & Higgins, 1995). Multiple studies have underscored the influence of teachers' computer self-efficacy on their technology integration behavior, for example, in the context of CALL 2.0 (Mei et al., 2018), e-learning (Khan et al., 2023), blended learning (Wong et al., 2016). In this study, AI self-efficacy refers to language teachers' confidence and belief in their ability to integrate AI for desirable educational outcomes. Some studies revealed significant relationships between AI self-efficacy and AI adoption intent. For instance, Sun et al. (2024) found that there existed a positive influence on AI self-efficacy on pre-service teachers' intention to use AI in STEM education. Similarly, Gado et al. (2022) indicated that students who rate their knowledge and skills of AI higher than their peers are more likely to use AI. The above ideas lead to develop the following hypothesis:

H4: AI self-efficacy can positively predict AI adoption intent.

AI-TPACK, performance expectancy, and effort expectancy

According to Mishra and Koehler (2006), TPACK refers to the knowledge required by teachers for effectively integrating technology into their teaching in any content area. TPACK encompasses three separate elements (content knowledge, pedagogical knowledge, and technological knowledge), and four combined elements (technological content knowledge, technology pedagogical knowledge, and technology pedagogical content knowledge). TPACK could be an important supplement to UTAUT because previous studies reveal TPACK's significant influence on teachers' willingness to integrate digital technologies into teaching (e.g., Al-Adwan et al., 2024; Bai et al., 2024). Drawing on the term TPACK by Mishra and Koehler (2006), An et al. (2023) proposed the concept of AI-TPACK which reflects essential knowledge (including content, pedagogy, AI) that educators need to integrate AI into teaching process. In the context of AI adoption in education, teachers with higher levels of AI-TPACK tend to perceive AI tools as more useful and easier to use in their teaching-related tasks, as evidenced in recent studies by Jain and Raghuram (2024), Thohir et al. (2023), and Sun et al. (2024). In other words, performance expectancy and effort expectancy are strongly impacted by AI-TPACK. In terms of the above discussions, two hypotheses are developed:

H5: AI-TPACK can positively predict performance expectancy.

H6: AI-TPACK can positively predict effort expectancy.

Facilitation, AI-TPACK, and AI self-efficacy

AI-TPACK reflects essential knowledge, including content, pedagogy, AI that educators need to integrate AI into teaching process (An et al., 2023). This conceptualization is crucial for modernizing the traditional TPACK framework by integrating AI-specific considerations. AI self-efficacy refers to language teachers' confidence and belief in their ability to integrate AI for desirable educational outcomes. Drawing on social cognitive theory (Bandura, 1986), suggesting that sufficient mastery is an important source of self-efficacy, it stands to reason that proficiency in AI-TPACK would increase teachers' confidence in using AI tools. In the context of technology, TPACK has a significant and positive direct effect on technology self-efficacy, as indicated in Al-Adwan et al. (2024) about technology use of high education teachers, Bai et al. (2024) and Durak (2021) about K-12 teachers' use of technology. In the context of AI, significant relationships between AI-TPACK and AI self-efficacy was found in Sun et al. (2024) about pre-service teachers' inclination to integrate AI into STEM education. Therefore, a high level of AI self-efficacy is informed by a high level of AI-TPACK. When teachers acquire adequate knowledge on how to integrate AI with teaching, they may understand the value of how technology enhances their teaching and students' learning and thus have confidence to use it. In terms of the above discussions, it is hypothesized as follows.

H7: AI-TPACK can positively predict AI self-efficacy.

According to Teo (2009), facilitation is defined as environmental factors that impact an individual's motivation to undertake a task. This concept is crucial in technology adoption, assessing the extent to which individuals perceive the infrastructure necessary to utilize technology effectively (Venkatesh et al., 2003). In this study, facilitation pertains to the perceived support that teachers receive from their organizations or institutions for using AI in teaching-related tasks. With the proliferation of new AI tools, teachers require substantial support to assimilate AI-related knowledge to improve teaching practices. Without adequate training and technical support, the effective use of emerging technologies is hindered. Supporting this idea, research by Al-Adwan et al. (2024) also highlighted the role of facilitation in enhancing TPACK among in-service and pre-service teachers. Additionally, Maipita et al. (2023) underscore various facilitation types, such as knowledge sharing, technical support, and praise, which contribute to increasing the TPACK capabilities of pre-service teachers in online learning environments. In the context of AI adoption in education, the literature indicates a positive impact of facilitation on AI-TPACK, as found in the study on pre-service teachers' use of virtual reality (Thohir et al., 2023) and English teachers' AI use in middle schools (An et al., 2023). Consequently, the hypothesis is stated below:

H8: Facilitation can positively predict AI-TPACK.

With all these hypotheses, a model is developed conceptually, and it is shown in Figure 1.

Methods

Sample and data collection

To answer the research question, data were gathered through an online questionnaire in May 2024. Within this period, 306 language teachers participated, and 276 valid responses were retained. 30 responses were removed from the survey due to incomplete data and outliers. Among 276 participants, 128 (46.4%) were male and 148 (53.6%) were female. In terms of age, the majority of respondents were between 25-30 years old (48.6%), followed by those aged 18-24 years (32.6%), 31-40 years (14.5%), and over 40 years (4.3%). Regarding teaching experience, the largest group had 4-10 years of experience (41.3%), while 32.6% had 1-3 years of experience, 15.2% had less than 1 year, 5.8% had 11-15 years, and 5.1% had more than 15 years of teaching experience. Educational qualifications among the respondents showed that 60.1% held a Bachelor's degree, 37.7% had a Master's degree, and 2.2% possessed a Doctorate. The frequency of AI use varied, with 41.3% reporting that they usually used AI, 39.9% sometimes used AI, 15.9% always used AI, and a small proportion rarely used AI (2.9%).

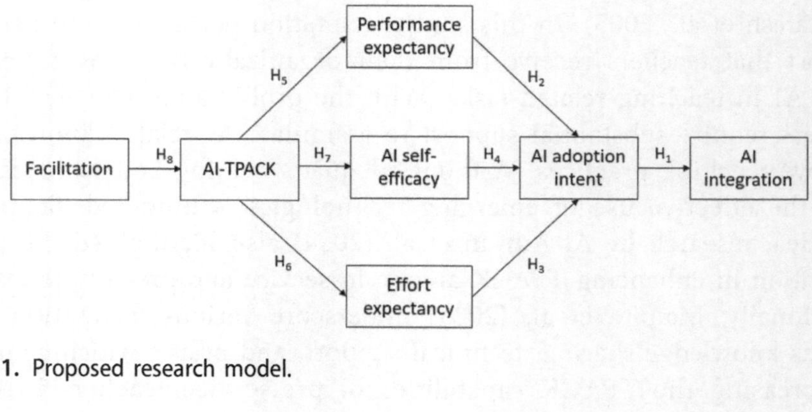

Figure 1. Proposed research model.

Instruments

The official survey consisted of three sections. The first section provided a brief introduction to the study, a consent form, and a screening question to check participants' prior experience with using AI chatbots for supporting teaching. The second section included a total of 22 items (see Supplementary Table): three items for facilitation (Ni & Cheung, 2023), five items for AI-TPACK (An et al., 2023), three items for AI self-efficacy (Li et al., 2019), four items for performance expectancy (An et al., 2023), three items for effort expectancy (Li et al., 2019), three items for AI adoption intent (Zhai & Ma, 2022), and one item for AI integration. The study utilized a five-point Likert scale, where responses ranged from 1 (strongly disagree) to 5 (strongly agree), to measure most variables. However, AI integration was assessed using a different five-point scale, ranging from 1 (never) to 5 (always). For AI integration, using single items is appropriate and should not be viewed as unsound because this construct is unidimensional and limited in scope (Fuchs & Diamantopoulos, 2009). The participants ended the survey after providing some demographic information in the final session.

Preceding the main survey, a pretest and a pilot test were performed to validate the measurement items. The Vietnamese version of the questionnaire was sent to the five specialists for pretesting, who included three researchers in educational technology and two senior language teachers who were well-versed in AI chatbots. Based on their responses, some minor modifications were made to improve the readability of the questionnaire. This pretest was followed by a pilot test with the participation of 50 EFL teachers who had experience using AI chatbots for supporting teaching tasks. Cronbach's alpha values of all items were above the minimum ratio of 0.7 (Hair et al., 2017). Therefore, the reliability of the measurement scale was achieved.

Data analysis

This study employed Partial Least Square-Structural Equation Modeling (PLS-SEM) for data analysis to enhance existing structural models. PLS-SEM was chosen for its several advantages, including its ability to handle multiple dependent and independent variables, address multivariate collinearity, and work effectively with small samples without the need for normal distribution (Hair et al., 2019). According to Barclay et al. (1995), the minimum sample size should equal 10 times the largest number of structural paths directed at a particular construct in the structural model. Since the model incorporates eight main paths, the sample size of 276 valid responses is well above the required threshold, making it ideal for

PLS estimation procedures. The study employed a two-step data analysis approach. First, the measurement model was assessed to verify construct reliability, convergent validity, and discriminant validity. In the second step, the structural model was evaluated to explore the relationships between independent and dependent variables. These analyses were conducted using SmartPLS version 3.3.

Findings

Common method bias (CMB)

Since this study employed a cross-sectional design based on self-reported data collection, common method bias (CMB) may have occurred. Multicollinearity tests should be conducted to ensure no common method biases in the data (Hair et al., 2019). Harman's one-factor test was also used to check common method variance in this study (Podsakoff et al., 2003). All 19 measurement items were required to converge under one single factor using the principal axis factoring method. The results in Table 1 revealed that the highest variance explained by a single factor was 35.413%, which is lower than the suggested threshold of 50%, confirming that the data is not suffering from any common method biases.

Measurement model assessment

In the measurement model, construct reliability, convergent validity, and discriminant validity were evaluated. Table 2 highlighted that almost all factor loadings were more significant than 0.70, ranging between 0.774 and 0.927, indicating significant and acceptable factor loadings (Hair et al., 2019). Cronbach's alpha was used to evaluate construct reliability with the minimum value of 0.7 (Hair et al., 2019). All constructs in the measurement model exhibited a Cronbach's alpha of 0.856 or higher, which is acceptable according to the threshold criteria. The Composite Reliability (CR) shows the construct internal consistency and the findings indicated that CR values exceeded the required threshold of 0.7 (Hair et al., 2019). In addition, average variance extracted (AVE) values of all constructs were reported to be higher than the accepted level of 0.5, achieving the convergent validity of the scale (Hair et al., 2019). Thus, our evaluations of standardized loadings, Cronbach's alpha, com-

Table 1. Harman's single factor test.

	Extraction sums of squared loadings		
Component	Total	% of variance	Cumulative %
1	7.791	35.413	35.413

Table 2. Convergent validity.

Items	Loading	α	CR	AVE
Facilitation		0.885	0.928	0.811
FAC1	0.902			
FAC2	0.927			
FAC3	0.873			
AI-TPACK		0.893	0.921	0.701
AIT1	0.822			
AIT2	0.803			
AIT3	0.846			
AIT4	0.867			
AIT5	0.848			
AI self-efficacy		0.860	0.914	0.781
AIS1	0.869			
AIS2	0.920			
AIS3	0.861			
Performance expectancy		0.869	0.911	0.720
PEE1	0.805			
PEE2	0.774			
PEE3	0.910			
PEE4	0.898			
Effort expectancy		0.916	0.947	0.856
EFE1	0.936			
EFE2	0.925			
EFE3	0.916			
AI adoption intent		0.856	0.912	0.776
ADI1	0.870			
ADI2	0.886			
ADI3	0.886			
AI integration AII	1.000	1.000	1.000	1.000

Notes. α = Cronbach's alpha, CR = composite reliability, AVE = average variance extracted.

Table 3. Discriminant validity – Heterotrait-Monotrait ratio of correlations.

Factors	AIT	EFE	FAC	ADI	AIS	AII	PEE
AIT							
EFE	0.533						
FAC	0.352	0.204					
ADI	0.447	0.501	0.189				
AIS	0.667	0.396	0.443	0.423			
AII	0.475	0.314	0.275	0.381	0.392		
PEE	0.533	0.611	0.143	0.623	0.371	0.435	

posite reliability, and AVE in Table 2 revealed that convergent validity and reliability were established satisfactorily in the measurement model.

Furthermore, the Heterotrait-Monotrait (HTMT) ratio of correlation, a higher boundary criterion, was applied for testing the discriminant validity as the second method. Table 3 suggested that all HTMT ratio test outcomes were lower than a threshold of .85 (Henseler et al., 2015), establishing the discriminant validity of the latent variables.

Structural model assessment

Table 4 showed that AI adoption intent had a significant relationship with AI integration ($\beta = 0.353$, $t = 4.827$), supporting H1. Performance expectancy and effort expectancy significantly influenced AI adoption intent; therefore, H2 ($\beta = 0.392$, $t = 6.119$) and H3 ($\beta = 0.171$, $t = 2.605$) were confirmed. The effect of AI self-efficacy on AI adoption intent was also found significant ($\beta = 0.174$, $t = 2.588$). Hence, H4 was empirically proved and supported. Furthermore, AI-TPACK demonstrated significant correlations with performance expectancy and effort expectancy, which supported H5 ($\beta = 0.471$, $t = 7.502$) and H6 ($\beta = 0.486$, $t = 7.572$). H7 was significant since AI-TPACK positively influenced AI self-efficacy ($\beta = 0.596$, $t = 12.348$). Likewise, facilitation had a significant relationship with AI-TPACK ($\beta = 0.321$, $t = 4.993$); thus, H8 was empirically verified.

In addition to path analysis, effect sizes (f^2) were also reported to understand a predictor's effect on an endogenous construct. Effect sizes of 0.02, 0.15, 0.35 should be interpreted small, medium, and large (Cohen, 1988). The model fit was assessedusing the standardized root mean square residual (SRMR) value, with an acceptable threshold is 0.08 (Henseler et al., 2015). The SRMR value of 0.059 obtained in our study indicated that the model fit criterion was satisfied.

Discussion

This study seeks to explore the key factors influencing language teachers' use of AI chatbots in educational environments. The research framework builds on the UTAUT model by integrating additional elements, including AI-TPACK and AI self-efficacy. The conceptual model tests eight hypotheses, refining the UTAUT to better explain users' acceptance of AI technologies. Significant findings from the path analysis are discussed in detail in the following sections.

This study reveals that AI adoption intent significantly influences the integration of AI chatbots in language teaching. This aligns with findings by Al Shamsi et al. (2022), Pillai et al. (2024), and Liu and Ma (2024), indicating that language teachers are more likely to use AI chatbots, such as ChatGPT, when they have a strong intent to adopt these tools. A high

Table 4. Relationships between direct effects of variables.

	Bootstrap 5000 times			Percentile 95%			
Paths	β	t-value	p-value	Lower	Upper	f^2	Result
H1: ADI → AII	0.353	4.827	0.000	0.207	0.492	0.142^s	Supported
H2: PEE → ADI	0.392	6.119	0.000	0.264	0.518	0.161^m	Supported
H3: EFE → ADI	0.171	2.605	0.009	0.039	0.296	0.030^s	Supported
H4: AIS → ADI	0.174	2.588	0.010	0.031	0.296	0.040^s	Supported
H5: AIT → PEE	0.471	7.502	0.000	0.344	0.589	0.286^m	Supported
H6: AIT → EFE	0.486	7.572	0.000	0.353	0.600	0.308^m	Supported
H7: AIT → AIS	0.596	12.348	0.000	0.500	0.688	0.550^l	Supported
H8: FAC → AIT	0.321	4.993	0.000	0.200	0.450	0.115^s	Supported

Note. s – small, m – medium, l – large; FAC = facilitation, AIT = AI-TPACK, AIS = AI self-efficacy, PEE = performance expectancy, EFE = effort expectancy, ADI = AI adoption intent, AII = AI integration.

level of AI adoption intent not only motivates teachers to explore these tools but also encourages them to proactively seek professional development opportunities, collaborate with colleagues, and share successful experiences. This proactive engagement fosters a deeper understanding of how AI can enhance their teaching methods, enabling them to refine their pedagogical approaches and seamlessly integrate AI technologies into their classrooms. Performance expectancy significantly predicts the intent to adopt AI among teachers. This finding is consistent with numerous prior studies on AI adoption in educational contexts, including those by An et al. (2023), Sun et al. (2024), and Thohir et al. (2023). These studies collectively indicate that when teachers perceive high performance expectancy—believing that AI can enhance their teaching efficiency and quality—they are more likely to express a strong intent to adopt such technologies. Effort expectancy is a significant factor influencing AI adoption intent among teachers. This finding is in line with previous research, such as studies by Choi et al. (2023), Sun et al. (2024), and Thohir et al. (2023), which emphasize that ease of use is a critical determinant in the acceptance of AI-driven chatbots. For teachers, the decision to adopt a particular AI tool is likely influenced by how quickly they can get started with the technology and how much effort it takes to become proficient in using it. If the technology requires substantial time and effort to master, it could become a significant barrier to adoption.

In addition, AI self-efficacy significantly influences the intent to adopt AI among teachers, which is similar to studies such as Gado et al. (2022) and Sun et al. (2024). When educators feel capable of navigating and implementing AI tools, they are more likely to explore and utilize these resources in their classrooms. Conversely, low self-efficacy may act as a barrier, preventing teachers from engaging with AI despite recognizing its potential benefits. The study also indicates that AI-TPACK strongly predicts AI self-efficacy among language teachers. Sun et al. (2024) supported that by enhancing teachers' knowledge at the intersection of technology, pedagogy, and content, educational institutions can boost AI self-efficacy, which in turn, may lead to greater adoption and more innovative use of AI in the classroom. Moreover, AI-TPACK significantly impacts both performance expectancy and effort expectancy among teachers. Consistent with earlier research (e.g., Jain & Raghuram, 2024; Thohir et al., 2023), the results suggest that when teachers possess strong AI-TPACK, they are more likely to perceive AI as both useful and easy to use in their teaching. Compared with the traditional technology, AI is driven by advanced algorithms and models that require specific technical knowledge for effective implementation. Without this knowledge, teachers may fail to recognize AI's potential, leading to hesitation in its adoption. Facilitation is crucial in fostering AI-TPACK development among teachers. The findings resonate with Vietnam's National Digital Transformation Strategy, emphasizing the importance of initiatives like teacher training programs, resource allocation, and technical support in empowering language educators to effectively build their AI-TPACK. An et al. (2023) also corroborate that facilitation, which includes access to resources, training, and ongoing support, assists teachers building the necessary knowledge and skills to effectively integrate AI into their teaching. Without adequate facilitation, teachers may struggle to develop AI-TPACK, hindering their ability to understand and utilize AI tools effectively.

Conclusion

Theoretical implications

This study makes a significant contribution to the growing body of knowledge on AI adoption in language education by providing novel theoretical insights. First, it integrates two key frameworks, UTAUT and TPACK, to present a comprehensive model that offers a deeper understanding of the factors driving AI adoption among language teachers. This integration bridges the gap between technology acceptance and AI-pedagogical-content knowledge, offering a fresh perspective on the complexities of AI integration in education. Second, the study highlights facilitation as a critical factor in the technology acceptance process, emphasizing how external support mechanisms, such as institutional resources, training, and collaboration, play a pivotal role not only in influencing teachers' initial intent to adopt AI, but also in ensuring its sustained integration into their pedagogical practices.

Practical implications

This study offers valuable insights for both teacher educators and classroom teachers, outlining a clear path for effective AI integration in language teaching. For teacher educators, the findings emphasize the importance of designing professional development programs that not only introduce theoretical concepts but also provide practical, hands-on experience with AI tools in real teaching scenarios. Crucially, these programs must ensure that teachers gain a comprehensive understanding across three key areas: AI, pedagogy, and content knowledge. By embedding AI-TPACK at the core of teacher training, educators can cultivate a deeper understanding of how these elements work together to enhance language instruction, empowering teachers to confidently apply AI in ways that improve student outcomes. For classroom teachers, the study emphasizes the need for a multifaceted approach, as AI integration in language teaching is not a one-size-fits-all solution. It underscores the importance of strong support systems, combining technical assistance, ongoing collaboration, and clear practical guidance on AI usage. Schools and institutions must create environments where teachers feel supported and capable of using AI effectively. Peer learning, success stories, and exposure to real-life AI applications in classrooms can further strengthen teachers' confidence, making AI adoption a natural and beneficial extension of their teaching practices.

The role of facilitation is particularly critical in Vietnam, where disparities in resources and infrastructure remain a challenge. Teachers in urban areas may have greater access to training and support, while those in rural settings often struggle with limited connectivity and fewer professional development opportunities. Introducing government-sponsored online platforms for AI training could bridge the gap between rural and urban educators. Additionally, fostering collaborative networks where teachers can share their experiences and best practices with AI tools, such as chatbots, would help build a community of practice that supports sustained adoption.

Limitations and future research

This study, while offering valuable insights into AI adoption among language teachers, has several limitations that should be acknowledged. Firstly, the data were collected through an online survey conducted solely among Vietnamese teachers, which may affect the generalizability of the findings. To enhance the robustness and applicability of future research, it is essential to include a more diverse sample across various countries and contexts. Secondly, the study relies solely on self-reported data, which may not accurately reflect actual behavior or experiences, as participants might provide desirable responses or may not fully recall their experiences. To address this limitation, future research should consider employing qualitative or mixed-method approaches, such as individual interviews or classroom observations to gain more insights into teachers' AI adoption. Thirdly, the current study primarily focuses on the overall impact of AI-TPACK on teachers' usage of AI chatbots. However, AI-TPACK is a multidimensional construct, encompassing various sub-dimensions of knowledge that interact in complex ways. Future research should delve deeper into these sub-dimensions, exploring how specific aspects of AI-TPACK, such as pedagogical knowledge, content knowledge, and technological knowledge, individually and collectively influence teachers' use of AI technologies.

Disclosure statement

No potential conflict of interest was reported by the author(s).

ORCID

Nguyen Hoang Mai Tram http://orcid.org/0000-0003-4796-3325

References

Ahmed, S. A., Suliman, M. A., Al-Qadri, A. H., & Zhang, W. (2024). Exploring the intention to use mobile learning applications among international students for Chinese language learning during the COVID-19 pandemic. *Journal of Applied Research in Higher Education*, *16*(4), 1093–1116. https://doi.org/10.1108/JARHE-01-2023-0012

Ajzen, I. (1991). The theory of planned behavior. *Organizational Behavior and Human Decision Processes*, *50*(2), 179–211. https://doi.org/10.1016/0749-5978(91)90020-T

Al-Adwan, A. S., Meet, R. K., Anand, S., Shukla, G. P., Alsharif, R., & Dabbaghia, M. (2024). Understanding continuous use intention of technology among higher education teachers in emerging economy: Evidence from integrated TAM, TPACK, and UTAUT model. *Studies in Higher Education*, 1–20. https://doi.org/10.1080/03075079.2024.2343955

Al Shamsi, J. H., Al-Emran, M., & Shaalan, K. (2022). Understanding key drivers affecting students' use of artificial intelligence-based voice assistants. *Education and Information Technologies*, *27*(6), 8071–8091. https://doi.org/10.1007/s10639-022-109473

An, X., Chai, C. S., Li, Y., Zhou, Y., Shen, X., Zheng, C., & Chen, M. (2023). Modeling English teachers' behavioral intention to use artificial intelligence in middle schools. *Education and Information Technologies*, *28*(5), 5187–5208. https://doi.org/10.1007/s10639-022-11286-z

Bai, X., Guo, R., & Gu, X. (2024). Effect of teachers' TPACK on their behavioral intention to use technology: Chain mediating effect of technology self-efficacy and attitude toward use. *Education and Information Technologies*, *29*(1), 1013–1032. https://doi.org/10.1007/s10639-023-12343-x

Bandura, A. (1986). *Social foundations of thought and action: A social cognitive theory.* Prentice-Hall.

Barclay, D. W., Higgins, C., & Thompson, R. (1995). The partial least squares approach to causal modeling: Personal computer adoption and use as illustration. *Technology Studies*, *2*(2), 285–309.

Bilquise, G., Ibrahim, S., & Salhieh, S. E. M. (2024). Investigating student acceptance of an academic advising chatbot in higher education institutions. *Education and Information Technologies*, *29*(5), 6357–6382. https://doi.org/10.1007/s10639-023-12076-x

Budhathoki, T., Zirar, A., Njoya, E. T., & Timsina, A. (2024). ChatGPT adoption and anxiety: A cross-country analysis utilising the unified theory of acceptance and use of technology (UTAUT). *Studies in Higher Education*, *49*(5), 831–846. https://doi.org/10.1080/03075079.2024.2333937

Chin, W. W., Marcolin, B. L., & Newsted, P. R. (2003). A partial least squares latent variable modeling approach for measuring interaction effects: Results from a Monte Carlo simulation study and an electronic-mail emotion/adoption study. *Information Systems Research*, *14*(2), 189–217. https://doi.org/10.1287/isre.14.2.189.16018

Choi, S., Jang, Y., & Kim, H. (2023). Influence of pedagogical beliefs and perceived trust on teachers' acceptance of educational artificial intelligence tools. *International Journal of Human–Computer Interaction*, *39*(4), 910–922. https://doi.org/10.1080/10447318.2022.2049145

Chun, T. W., & Yunus, M. M. (2023). Factors affecting Malaysian ESL teachers' behavioral intentions for technology use in the post-COVID-19 era. *Frontiers in Psychology, 14*, 1127272. https://doi.org/10.3389/fpsyg.2023.1127272

Cohen, J. (1988). Statistical power analysis for the behavioral sciences. Lawrence Earlbaum Associates. https://doi.org/10.1234/12345678

Compeau, D. R., & Higgins, C. A. (1995). Computer self-efficacy: Development of a measure and initial test. *MIS Quarterly, 19*(2), 189–211. https://doi.org/10.2307/249688

Davis, F. D. (1989). Perceived usefulness, perceived ease of use, and user acceptance of information technology. *MIS Quarterly, 13*(3), 319–340. https://doi.org/10.2307/249008

Divekar, R. R., Drozdal, J., Chabot, S., Zhou, Y., Su, H., Chen, Y., Zhu, H., Hendler, J. A., & Braasch, J. (2022). Foreign language acquisition via artificial intelligence and extended reality: Design and evaluation. *Computer Assisted Language Learning, 35*(9), 2332–2360. https://doi.org/10.1080/09588221.2021.1879162

Durak, H. Y. (2021). Modeling of relations between K-12 teachers' TPACK levels and their technology integration self-efficacy, technology literacy levels, attitudes toward technology and usage objectives of social networks. *Interactive Learning Environments, 29*(7), 1–27. https://doi.org/10.1080/10494820.2019.1619591

Fagan, M. H. (2019). Factors influencing student acceptance of mobile learning in higher education. *Computers in the Schools, 36*(2), 105–121. https://doi.org/10.1080/07380569.2019.1603051

Fishbein, M., & Ajzen, I. (1975). *Belief, attitude, intention, and behavior: An Introduction to theory and research.* Addison-Wesley.

Fuchs, C., & Diamantopoulos, A. (2009). Using single-item measures for construct measurement in management research: Conceptual issues and application guidelines. *Die Betrieb-Swirtschaft, 69*(2), 195–210.

Gado, S., Kempen, R., Lingelbach, K., & Bipp, T. (2022). Artificial intelligence in psychology: How can we enable psychology students to accept and use artificial intelligence? *Psychology Learning & Teaching, 21*(1), 37–56. https://doi.org/10.1177/14757257211037149

Habibi, A., Riady, Y., Samed Al-Adwan, A., & Awni Albelbisi, N. (2023). Beliefs and knowledge for pre-service teachers' technology integration during teaching practice: An extended theory of planned behavior. *Computers in the Schools, 40*(2), 107–132. https://doi.org/10.1080/07380569.2022.2124752

Hair, J. F., Risher, J. J., Sarstedt, M., & Ringle, C. M. (2019). When to use and how to report the results of PLS-SEM. *European Business Review, 31*(1), 2–24. https://doi.org/10.1108/EBR-11-2018-0203

Hair, J. F., Sarstedt, M., Ringle, C. M., & Gudergan, S. P. (2017). *Advanced issues in partial least squares structural equation modeling.* Sage. https://doi.org/10.3926/oss.37

Henseler, J., Ringle, C. M., & Sarstedt, M. (2015). A new criterion for assessing discriminant validity in variance-based structural equation modeling. *Journal of the Academy of Marketing Science, 43*(1), 115–135. https://doi.org/10.1007/s11747-0140403-8

Hsu, L. (2023). EFL learners' self-determination and acceptance of LMOOCs: The UTAUT model. *Computer Assisted Language Learning, 36*(7), 1177–1205. https://doi.org/10.1080/09588221.2021.1976210

Jain, K. K., & Raghuram, J. N. V. (2024). Gen-AI integration in higher education: Predicting intentions using SEM-ANN approach. *Education and Information Technologies, 29*(13), 17169–17209. https://doi.org/10.1007/s10639-024-12506-4

Kenny, D. A. (2018). Moderator variables: Introduction. Retrieved June 2024, from http://davidakenny.net/cm/moderation.htm

Khan, M. J., Reddy, L. K. V., Khan, J., Narapureddy, B. R., Vaddamanu, S. K., Alhamoudi, F. H., Vyas, R., Gurumurthy, V., Altijani, A. A. G., & Chaturvedi, S. (2023). Challenges of E-learning: Behavioral intention of academicians to use E-learning during COVID-19 crisis. *Journal of Personalized Medicine, 13*(3), 555. https://doi.org/10.3390/jpm13030555

Kohnke, L., Moorhouse, B. L., & Zou, D. (2023). ChatGPT for language teaching and learning. *RELC Journal, 54*(2), 537–550. https://doi.org/10.1177/00336882231162868

Li, R., Meng, Z., Tian, M., Zhang, Z., Ni, C., & Xiao, W. (2019). Examining EFL learners' individual antecedents on the adoption of automated writing evaluation in China. *Computer Assisted Language Learning, 32*(7), 784–804. https://doi.org/10.1080/09588221.2018.1540433

Li, T., Zou, D., Weng, X., Wang, M., Xie, H., & Wang, F. L. (2020). Acceptance and implications of smartphones for informal language learning in foreign study tours. *International Journal of Mobile Learning and Organisation, 14*(4), 456–477. https://doi.org/10.1504/IJMLO.2020.110783

Liu, G., & Ma, C. (2024). Measuring EFL learners' use of ChatGPT in informal digital learning of English based on the technology acceptance model. *Innovation in Language Learning and Teaching, 18*(2), 125–138. https://doi.org/10.1080/17501229.2023.2240316

Lo, C. K. (2023). What is the impact of ChatGPT on education? A rapid review of the literature. *Education Sciences, 13*(4), 410. https://doi.org/10.3390/educsci13040410

Maipita, I., Rahman Dongoran, F., Husrizal Syah, D., & Hafiz Sagala, G. (2023). TPACK, organizational support, and technostress in explaining teacher performance during fully online learning. *Journal of Information Technology Education: Research, 22*, 41–70. https://doi.org/10.28945/5069

Mei, B., Brown, G. T. L., & Teo, T. (2018). Toward an understanding of preservice English as a foreign language teachers' acceptance of computer-assisted language learning 2.0 in the People's Republic of China. *Journal of Educational Computing Research, 56*(1), 74–104. https://doi.org/10.1177/0735633117700144

Mishra, P., & Koehler, M. J. (2006). Technological pedagogical content knowledge: A framework for teacher knowledge. *Teachers College Record: The Voice of Scholarship in Education, 108*(6), 1017–1054. https://doi.org/10.1111/j.1467-9620.2006.00684.x

Mohamed, A. M. (2024). Exploring the potential of an AI-based Chatbot (ChatGPT) in enhancing English as a foreign language (EFL) teaching: Perceptions of EFL faculty members. *Education and Information Technologies, 29*(3), 3195–3217. https://doi.org/10.1007/s10639-023-11917-z

Ni, A., & Cheung, A. (2023). Understanding secondary students' continuance intention to adopt AI-powered intelligent tutoring system for English learning. *Education and Information Technologies, 28*(3), 3191–3216. https://doi.org/10.1007/s10639-02211305-z

Nie, J., Zheng, C., Zeng, P., Zhou, B., Lei, L., & Wang, P. (2020). Using the theory of planned behavior and the role of social image to understand mobile English learning check-in behavior. *Computers & Education, 156*, 103942. https://doi.org/10.1016/j.compedu.2020.103942

Ogegbo, A. A., Penn, M., Ramnarain, U., Pila, O., Van Der Westhuizen, C., Mdlalose, N., Moser, I., Hlosta, M., & Bergamin, P. (2024). Exploring pre-service teachers' intentions of adopting and using virtual reality classrooms in science education. *Education and Information Technologies, 29*(15), 20299–20316. https://doi.org/10.1007/s10639-024-12664-5

Pillai, R., Sivathanu, B., Metri, B., & Kaushik, N. (2024). Students' adoption of AI-based teacher-bots (T-bots) for learning in higher education. *Information Technology & People, 37*(1), 328–355. https://doi.org/10.1108/ITP-02-2021-0152

Podsakoff, P. M., MacKenzie, S. B., Lee, J. Y., & Podsakoff, N. P. (2003). Common method biases in behavioral research: A critical review of the literature and recommended remedies. *The Journal of Applied Psychology, 88*(5), 879–903. https://doi.org/10.1037/00219010.88.5.879

Rahman, T., Kim, Y. S., Noh, M., & Lee, C. K. (2021). A study on the determinants of social media-based learning in higher education. *Educational Technology Research and Development*, *69*(2), 1325–1351. https://doi.org/10.1007/s11423-021-09987-2

Raza, S. A., Qazi, W., Khan, K. A., & Salam, J. (2021). Social isolation and acceptance of the learning management system (LMS) in the time of COVID-19 pandemic: An expansion of the UTAUT model. *Journal of Educational Computing Research*, *59*(2), 183–208. https://doi.org/10.1177/0735633120960421

Rudolph, J., Tan, S., & Tan, S. (2023). ChatGPT: Bullshit spewer or the end of traditional assessments in higher education? *Journal of Applied Learning and Teaching*, *6*(1), 342–363. https://doi.org/10.37074/jalt.2023.6.1.9

Shahid, M. K., Zia, T., Bangfan, L., Iqbal, Z., & Ahmad, F. (2024). Exploring the relationship of psychological factors and adoption readiness in determining university teachers' attitude on AI-based assessment systems. *The International Journal of Management Education*, *22*(2), 100967. https://doi.org/10.1016/j.ijme.2024.100967

Shen, F., Liang, L., & Feng, Y. (2023). A study on factors influencing Chinese undergraduate EFL learners' self-directed use of mobile English learning resources. *Frontiers in Psychology*, *14*, 1189055. https://doi.org/10.3389/fpsyg.2023.1189055

Sun, F., Tian, P., Sun, D., Fan, Y., & Yang, Y. (2024). Pre-service teachers' inclination to integrate AI into STEM education: Analysis of influencing factors. *British Journal of Educational Technology*, *55*(6), 2574–2596. https://doi.org/10.1111/bjet.13469

Teo, T. (2009). Modelling technology acceptance in education: A study of pre-service teachers. *Computers & Education*, *52*(2), 302–312. https://doi.org/10.1016/j.compedu.2008.08.006

Teo, T. (2011). Factors influencing teachers' intention to use technology: Model development and test. *Computers & Education*, *57*(4), 2432–2440. https://doi.org/10.1016/j.compedu.2011.06.008

Teo, T., Sang, G., Mei, B., & Hoi, C. (2019). Investigating pre-service teachers' acceptance of web 2.0 technologies in their future teaching: A Chinese perspective. *Interactive Learning Environments*, *27*(4), 530–546. https://doi.org/10.1080/10494820.2018.1489290

Thohir, M. A., Ahdhianto, E., Mas'ula, S., April Yanti, F., & Sukarelawan, M. I. (2023). The effects of TPACK and facility condition on preservice teachers' acceptance of virtual reality in science education course. *Contemporary Educational Technology*, *15*(2), ep407. https://doi.org/10.30935/cedtech/12918

Tram, N. H. M., & Tran-Thanh, V. (2024). The role of supportive environments in shaping EFL teachers' adoption of ChatGPT In P. H. Bui & E. Namaziandost (Eds.), *Innovations in technologies for language teaching and learning*. Springer. https://doi.org/10.1007/978-3-031-63447-5_4

Tram, N. H. M., Nguyen, T. T., & Tran, C. D. (2024). ChatGPT as a tool for self-learning English among EFL learners: A multi-methods study. *System*, *127*, 103528. https://doi.org/10.1016/j.system.2024.103528

Ustun, A. B., Karaoglan-Yilmaz, F. G., Yilmaz, R., Ceylan, M., & Uzun, O. (2024). Development of UTAUT-based augmented reality acceptance scale: A validity and reliability study. *Education and Information Technologies*, *29*(9), 11533–11554. https://doi.org/10.1007/s10639-023-12321-3

Venkatesh, V., Morris, M. G., Davis, G. B., & Davis, F. D. (2003). User acceptance of information technology: Toward a unified view. *MIS Quarterly*, *27*(3), 425–478. https://doi.org/10.2307/30036540

Venkatesh, V., Thong, J. Y., & Xu, X. (2012). Consumer acceptance and use of information technology: Extending the unified theory of acceptance and use of technology. *MIS Quarterly*, *36*(1), 157–178. https://doi.org/10.2307/41410412

Wiangkham, A., & Vongvit, R. (2024). Exploring the drivers for the adoption of metaverse technology in engineering education using PLS-SEM and ANFIS. *Education and Information Technologies*, *29*(6), 7385–7412. https://doi.org/10.1007/s10639-023-12127-3

Wong, K. T., Hamzah, S. G., Goh, P. S. C., & Yeop, M. A. (2016). Blended e-learning acceptance as smart pedagogical tools: An initial study in Malaysia. *Turkish Online Journal of Educational Technology*, *15*(4), 25–31.

Xiaohong, L., Jun, Z., Xiaoming, C., & Beina, Z. (2024). A study on behavioral intentions of artificial intelligence learning platform: Comparing the perspectives of teachers and students. *Interactive Learning Environments*, 1–21. https://doi.org/10.1080/10494820.2024.2343752

Xu, X., & Thien, L. M. (2024). Unleashing the power of perceived enjoyment: Exploring Chinese undergraduate EFL learners' intention to use ChatGPT for English learning. *Journal of Applied Research in Higher Education*. https://doi.org/10.1108/JARHE-12-2023-0555

Yang, L., & Li, R. (2024). ChatGPT for L2 learning: Current status and implications. *System*, *124*, 103351. https://doi.org/10.1016/j.system.2024.103351

Zhai, N., & Ma, X. (2022). Automated writing evaluation (AWE) feedback: A systematic investigation of college students' acceptance. *Computer Assisted Language Learning*, *35*(9), 2817–2842. https://doi.org/10.1080/09588221.2021.1897019

Zou, C., Li, P., & Jin, L. (2022). Integrating smartphones in EFL classrooms: Students' satisfaction and perceived learning performance. *Education and Information Technologies*, *27*(9), 12667–12688. https://doi.org/10.1007/s10639-022-11103-7

Assessing the Efficacy of Intelligent Tutoring Systems in Language Teacher Education: A Quantitative Study

Soumya Sankar Ghosh

ABSTRACT

This research investigates the influence of Intelligent Tutoring Systems (ITS) on the training of language educators. In order to analyze the data, we utilized structural equation modeling. We focused on both inexperienced and experienced educators. Our objective was to determine the factors that enable ITS to operate effectively, in terms of student results and instructional approaches. The data was collected through the use of questionnaires, student test scores, and classroom observations. This gave us a precise depiction of the utilization of ITS, which leads us to conclude that ITS offer significant that this tutoring system offers significant benefits in evaluating both students' performance and teachers' instructional techniques. In this context, the research underscores the potential of ITS to substantially enhance the training of language educators.

Introduction

The field of language teaching has been in a perpetual state of evolution since its inception and in the process of that it adapts to accommodate new technologies. Intelligent Tutoring Systems (henceforth ITS) have become influential educational aids in recent years. These systems utilize artificial intelligence to deliver tailored training and feedback, adjusting to the individual needs of each student. ITS has the capability to replicate individualized tutoring, providing customized assistance that can improve educational results. This technology has great potential in the field of language teaching since it has the ability to enhance proficiency and fluency through personalized attention. Although the potential advantages of this have been extensively studied in the field of education as a whole (Ma et al., 2014), their specific effects on language teacher education have not been thoroughly investigated. Language educators have a vital role in molding the educational encounters of their students. So, research into education makes it clear that training and professional growth for teachers need to be a top priority. In order to be successful, teacher education programs must give teachers the knowledge and skills they need to use modern technology like ITS in the classroom. This study aims to close a gap in the existing literature by investigating the integration of these systems into language teacher education and identifying the factors that influence their success.

The growing trend in education toward the incorporation of data-driven technologies and Artificial Intelligence (AI) in teaching and learning is reflected in the increasing ubiquity of ITS. If we look closely, we will see that these technologies have the potential to revolutionize traditional teaching practices, enhancing training by increasing efficacy, customization, and interaction. These systems leverage advances in cognitive science, machine learning, and natural language processing to deliver individualized instruction suited to each learner's unique needs (VanLehn, 2011). They can provide immediate feedback, track students' progress, and modify the content to challenge pupils in the right way. These attributes are especially beneficial in language education, as pupils often benefit from immediate feedback and customized practice. But in spite of its potential (Koedinger et al., 1997), it is important to mention here that the use of it in language teacher education faces several problems. A significant obstacle, one can think of, is the dearth of actual evidence regarding their efficacy in this particular context. So, before the integration of ITS into teachers' training programs, it is necessary to ensure these diverse and complex requirements.

Furthermore, the efficacy of ITS is very much dependent upon other elements, such as the caliber of the technology, the integration's design, and the willingness of teachers and students to adopt and utilize these tools. Prior research has indicated that the incorporation of technology into education frequently encounters obstacles such as insufficient training, insufficient support, and reluctance to embrace change (Ertmer & Ottenbreit-Leftwich, 2010). Hence, it is imperative to comprehend the circumstances in which ITS can be seamlessly included into language teacher education.

Keeping all these things in mind, the current study delves into the efficacy of ITS within the domain of language teacher education. To achieve this, it sets out three primary objectives, which are as follows:

- To pinpoint the key factors that influence the effectiveness of ITS in this specialized educational context. This involves examining both technological aspects and contextual variables that may affect implementation and outcomes.

- To explore how the integration of ITS impacts the instructional practices of language teachers, focusing on both pre-service and in-service educators. We are particularly interested in understanding how ITS can enhance teaching methodologies, improve lesson planning, and support ongoing professional development.
- To assess the broader effects of ITS on the student learning outcomes. By analyzing changes in student performance, we hope to evaluate the overall impact of ITS on language education.

These objectives are addressed through three research questions:

1. What are the key factors that influence the effectiveness of ITS in language teacher education?
2. How does the integration of ITS impact the instructional practices of pre-service and in-service language teachers?
3. What is the effect of ITS on student learning outcomes in language education?

By addressing these research questions, the study aims to provide comprehensive insights that can guide educators, policymakers, and researchers in effectively incorporating ITS into language teacher education programs.

Literature review

Intelligent Tutoring Systems (ITS) are a notable breakthrough in educational technology, created to offer individualized instruction and feedback to learners. These systems utilize artificial intelligence to imitate the abilities of human tutors, adjusting to the specific requirements of pupils to improve learning results. A system may continuously assess students' performance, provide rapid feedback, and adjust instructional approaches accordingly. The integration of natural language processing, machine learning, and cognitive science principles enables this dynamic interaction (VanLehn, 2011). The diagnostic capacity is one of the fundamental capabilities of ITS. Students can learn about their strengths and weaknesses by examining their responses and interactions. ITS has the ability to give tailored educational materials that address specific areas of learning insufficiency. As an example, if a student is having trouble with a subject, ITS could give them more practice problems or change the level of difficulty of the tasks to match their skill level (Ma et al., 2014). This individualized approach guarantees that students receive assignments that are at the appropriate degree of difficulty and assistance, which is essential for efficient learning.

In addition, ITS can replicate the interactive and conversational aspects of human tutoring. They have the ability to include pupils in interactive discussions, by asking questions, giving hints, and promoting critical thinking. This not only facilitates the acquisition of knowledge but also enhances the critical thinking and problem-solving abilities (Graesser et al., 2012). In addition, they also monitor and analyze learning patterns over a period of time, providing valuable information on student advancement and identifying areas that need additional focus. By utilizing a data-driven approach, educators are able to make well-informed judgments on instructional tactics and interventions. These systems have been implemented in diverse educational settings, ranging from primary and secondary schools to universities and vocational training. In the field of mathematics, systems such as *Cognitive Tutor* have shown notable enhancements in student performance through the provision of personalized problem-solving activities (Koedinger et al., 1997). In the field of science education, ITS have been employed to support inquiry-based learning. This approach enables students to investigate scientific topics by engaging in guided discovery and experimentation (VanLehn et al., 2003). ITS possess a high degree of versatility and adaptability, rendering them highly important instruments for enriching learning experiences in various topics and educational levels.

ITS, as the paper points out here, provide a sophisticated method of delivering personalized, interactive, and adaptive training. Their aptitude for identifying learning requirements, delivering customized assistance, and monitoring advancement renders them a formidable asset in the field of education. With the increasing integration of technology in learning environments, the importance of ITS is expected to grow. This is especially true in fields such as language teaching, where personalized attention can greatly influence learning results.

ITS in language education: Previous studies and their findings

When it comes to language learning, where you need personalized feedback and practice, ITS is a good fit. Previous research has shown us that ITS in the field of language education, not only helps in encompassing vocabulary acquisition, but also in writing skills, and pronunciation practice. These studies shed light on the possible advantages and disadvantages of incorporating ITS into language learning contexts. In this particular context, ITS has demonstrated particular potential in the field of language acquisition. *Robo-Sensei* and similar systems have been utilized to assist second-language learners of Japanese in enhancing their vocabulary through interactive exercises and quizzes (Holland et al., 2013). It assesses the learner's language level proficiency, and in addition to that it offers suitable difficulties and instant feedback. Nakata (2011), in this situation, notes that engaging in individualized practice can result in notable enhancements in the ability to remember and use language.

ITS can have a significant influence on writing skills. Automated Writing Evaluation (AWE) systems, such as *Grammarly* and *Criterion*, utilize natural language processing to deliver immediate comments on grammar, syntax, and style. These programs assist learners in enhancing their writing by detecting faults and proposing enhancements. Studies have shown that using AWE systems regularly can improve writing skills by promoting repeated editing and self-correction (Warschauer & Grimes, 2008). In addition, Intelligent Tutoring Systems (ITS) can offer enhanced support for intricate writing assignments by giving scaffolded assistance. This guidance aids learners in organizing their writings and constructing cohesive arguments (Stevenson & Phakiti, 2014). In addition to writing, ITS has been successfully utilized in the domain of pronunciation practice. Automatic Speech Recognition (ASR) technologies, such as *NativeAccent*, are utilized to examine the pronunciation of learners and offer corrected feedback. These systems have the ability to identify minor faults in pronunciation and provide targeted workouts to enhance articulation and fluency. Research has indicated that focused practice can result in significant enhancements in pronunciation, enabling learners to attain speech patterns that resemble those of native speakers (Chiu et al., 2007).

These applications of ITS in specific language skills underscore the broader potential of ITS to support educators and learners alike, extending beyond student practice to enhance the effectiveness of teacher preparation. Recognizing this potential, recent developments have seen the integration of ITS into language teacher training programs to equip educators with the tools and strategies needed to implement technology-driven instruction. In this context, specific ITS tools such as *Cognitive Tutor* and *TutorMate* have emerged as influential educational aids, particularly for the participants in this study, who were already familiar with these systems. *Cognitive Tutor*, developed by researchers including Anderson, et al., (1995), has been widely recognized for its application in mathematics education, utilizing a cognitive model to offer personalized instruction and practice. Studies on *Cognitive Tutor* have shown its effectiveness in improving students' problem-solving skills by adapting to individual learning needs, as highlighted by Ritter et al. (2007). Although originally designed for subjects such as mathematics, the principles of *Cognitive Tutor* have implications for language education, particularly in its capacity to provide adaptive feedback and support structured learning. This feature makes it a valuable tool for in-service teachers, who can use its adaptability to tailor instruction to diverse student needs, thereby enhancing language instruction through data-driven insights. Conversely, *TutorMate* has been extensively employed to support literacy and language learning, particularly for younger students. Research by Guernsey and Levine (2015) explains how *TutorMate* engages students in literacy development through digital media, offering one-on-one tutoring sessions that target foundational reading skills. The system's use of interactive exercises and personalized reading support aligns with the needs of pre-service teachers, who benefit from guided instruction on essential language teaching skills. Stark (2016) further emphasizes that *TutorMate* operates as an evidence-based tool, supporting literacy through individualized tutoring, which complements early education initiatives.

While the advantages of ITS in language instruction are well-documented, several challenges hinder their broader application. A primary obstacle is the need for high-quality content and accurate language models. Developing effective ITS requires a deep understanding of language acquisition processes and the ability to create engaging pedagogically sound content. Additionally, the success of these systems relies on their seamless integration into existing educational frameworks. To achieve this, teachers need proper training to use these technologies effectively and incorporate them smoothly into their instructional practices (Blake, 2013). Most studies on ITS tools like *Cognitive Tutor* and *TutorMate* have focused on their use with primary or secondary students rather than on training pre-service or in-service teachers. This lack of recent research on their effectiveness and integration within teacher education programs underscores the need for studies that assess their impact on language teacher readiness, adaptability to diverse classroom contexts, and overall effectiveness in developing instructional skills.

Challenges in language teacher education: current issues and how ITS can address them

Many problems in the field of language teacher education make it hard to train teachers well. The necessity for a comprehensive training that incorporates not only subject matter expertise but also instructional techniques and cultural proficiencies is a critical concern. Language educators must have the requisite abilities to effectively manage classes with a diverse student body, integrate technology into their teaching, and employ efficient instructional methods. Nevertheless, conventional teacher education programs occasionally fail to provide comprehensive instruction in this multidimensional aspect (Richards, 2008). The inconsistent level of teacher preparation is a significant impediment. Practical skills are often overlooked in numerous teacher education programs, which prioritize theoretical knowledge. As a result, inexperienced educators often begin their careers in the classroom without the necessary practical experience or the ability to implement effective teaching methodologies. In the field of language instruction, where instructors are confronted with substantial demands, the discrepancy between theory and practice can lead to feelings of dissatisfaction and exhaustion (Freeman & Johnson, 1998). Another issue is the limited availability of professional development opportunities for instructors who are currently employed. In order to remain informed about the latest educational research, technologies, and instructional methodologies, instructors must engage in continuous professional development. However, numerous educators are unable to access these opportunities due to factors such as geographical constraints, insufficient resources, and a lack of time. This limitation can impede the ability of instructors to improve their methodology and adapt to changes in the educational environment (Darling-Hammond et al., 2009).

ITS, in this regard, offers a potential remedy to these challenges. As already discussed above, providing personalized instruction and feedback has the potential to enhance the quality of teacher education for both pre-service and in-service educators. The provision of simulated teaching experiences by ITS can facilitate the connection between theoretical knowledge and practical application for pre-service instructors. These systems provide instructors with the opportunity to practice classroom management, lesson planning, and instructional delivery in a secure and regulated setting. Teachers' preparedness for actual educational environments can be improved by participating in practical exercises, which can increase their self-assurance and proficiency (Anderson et al., 1995). On the other hand, those who are currently employed may receive ongoing professional development from ITS. These systems offer personalized learning modules that concentrate on specific areas of need, allowing instructors to participate in continuous learning at their own pace. In addition, schools and colleges could ensure that educators receive the requisite resources and support to remain proficient and current by integrating ITS into professional development programs (Desimone, 2009). The aforementioned systems are also helpful in alleviating the issue of teacher isolation. Occasionally, language instructors encounter circumstances in which they have limited opportunities to engage in collaborative efforts and receive assistance from their colleagues. ITS can provide a virtual platform for collaboration, allowing teachers to engage with colleagues, exchange information, and partake in professional development communities. The establishment of this connection has the potential to enhance the morale of educators and reduce feelings of seclusion by fostering a sense of inclusion and assistance (Vescio et al., 2008).

Despite the potential of ITS to address these challenges, empirical evidence is still necessary to confirm its effectiveness in language teacher education. The literature is devoid of information regarding the specific impact of these systems on teacher training and professional development, even though previous studies in other areas have identified the potential benefits of using them. There is a need for research that examines the successful incorporation of ITS into teacher education programs and its influence on student outcomes and teaching practices. The scarcity of research in this field serves as a compelling reason to investigate the utilization of Structural Equation Modeling (henceforth, SEM) to evaluate the impact of ITS on the education of language teachers. A robust framework for investigating the complex relationships between factors related to the integration of these systems, teacher training, and student academic achievement is provided by SEM. This research endeavors to rectify this deficiency by employing SEM to evaluate the efficacy of ITS in the education of language teachers, thereby providing valuable insights for educators, policymakers, and researchers.

Structural Equation Modeling (SEM): overview and relevance in educational research

Structural Equation Modeling (SEM) is a robust statistical method employed in educational research to examine intricate connections among variables. This feature makes it especially valuable for studying complex phenomena such as the influence of ITS on language teacher education (Kline, 2023). It integrates factor analysis and multiple regression elements, allowing for the simultaneous examination of several interdependent connections. For the current work, SEM is important for its capacity to integrate latent variables, which are unobservable constructs derived from the data. For instance, when examining ITS, one can incorporate latent variables like "teacher readiness" or "student engagement" into the model, which enhances the comprehension of the various aspects that impact educational results (Byrne, 2013). The procedure of performing SEM encompasses multiple stages. Initially, a theoretical framework is constructed by drawing upon established literature and theories. This model delineates the anticipated associations among variables. Subsequently, data is gathered and utilized to approximate the parameters of the model. Afterwards, the model's adequacy is evaluated using different statistical measures, including the Chi-square test, Comparative Fit Index (CFI), and Root Mean Square Error of Approximation (RMSEA). An accurate model fit suggests that the proposed associations align with the observed data (Black et al., 2010).

Within the scope of this investigation, Structural Equation Modeling is advantageous due to its capacity to analyze intricate data and evaluate theoretical frameworks. For instance, in assessing the efficacy of ITS in language teacher education, SEM can be employed to analyze the interplay between many elements, such as teacher attitudes toward technology, the quality of ITS material, and student involvement, in order to determine their impact on learning results. This comprehensive approach offers more profound insights compared to conventional statistical methods, which frequently analyze variables independently (Wang & Wang, 2019). Moreover, it can take into consideration the presence of measurement error, hence improving the accuracy and consistency of the results. Measurement error in educational research can stem from multiple factors, including mistakes in survey replies or inconsistencies in observational data. By explicitly incorporating these mistakes into the model, structural equation modeling (SEM) yields more precise estimates of the relationships between variables, resulting in more reliable and conclusive findings (Brown, 2015). The significance of SEM in examining ITS and language teacher education is quite important. The process of integrating it encompasses a multitude of interrelated components, encompassing technological, pedagogical, and contextual aspects. The statistical modeling further enables researchers to untangle intricate connections and pinpoint the crucial factors that contribute to success. It also provides guidance in the development and implementation of language teaching and learning tools, ensuring that they are customized to address the specific requirements of teachers and learners (Black et al., 2010). SEM, thus, is an useful tool in educational research. It provides a comprehensive method for examining intricate interactions between factors. The capacity to include hidden variables, manage inaccuracies in measurement, and evaluate theoretical frameworks makes it especially appropriate for examining the complex characteristics of integrating ITS in language teacher education.

Methodology

Research design

This study employed a correlational design to first identify the key factors that influence the effectiveness of ITS in language teacher education and then examine the extent to which the integration of ITS impacts instructional practices and student learning outcomes. The correlational approach allows us to explore relationships among variables without manipulating them, making it suitable for studying real-world interactions between ITS, teaching efficacy, and student performance. To achieve these objectives, data collection included surveys (as detailed in Appendix A), classroom observations, and the examination of student performance records. Surveys gathered quantitative data on teachers' experiences, attitudes, and perceived ease of use and usefulness of ITS. Classroom observations provided context on ITS application in instructional settings, focusing on differences in usage between pre-service and in-service teachers. Finally, student performance data, including standardized test scores and grades, assessed ITS's impact on learning outcomes.

Data were analyzed using Structural Equation Modeling to determine the strength and significance of relationships among variables, such as perceived usefulness and ease of use, teaching efficacy, and student performance. SEM, as a correlational technique, facilitated the examination of both direct and indirect effects, offering insights into ITS's role in shaping instructional effectiveness and student achievement.

Participants

The study includes language teachers from various educational institutions, including pre-service and in-service. The purpose of selecting participants is to encompass a wide range of experiences and viewpoints about the utilization of Intelligent Tutoring Systems (ITS) in language education. Pre-service teachers are instructed on the incorporation of ITS into teacher training programs, whilst in-service teachers offer perspectives on the actual implementation and difficulties of ITS in real-life classroom environments. The study recruited a total of 200 language teachers from educational institutions across India, including states such as Maharashtra, Madhya Pradesh, West Bengal, Tamil Nadu, and Uttar Pradesh, to capture a diverse range of perspectives on the utilization of Intelligent Tutoring Systems in language education. Participants were evenly divided into 100 pre-service and 100 in-service teachers. Pre-service teachers were selected from teacher training programs at various universities and colleges across these states, ensuring a representative sample of future educators. In-service teachers were recruited from primary and secondary schools and language institutes, covering both urban and rural areas to provide a broad perspective on ITS implementation in real-world classroom environments. This varied sample enables a thorough examination of the influence of ITS on various phases of teacher growth and educational environments. To get a comprehensive of the participants, consider the following table (Table 1).

Table 1. Participants details.

Participant Group	Number of Participants	Years of Experience (M, SD)	Grade Levels	Gender: Female (%)	Gender: Male (%)
Pre-service Teachers	100	0 (Training Phase)	N/A	52	48
In-service Teachers	100	15.3 (SD = 6.2)	Primary, Secondary	52	48

Note: Years of experience (M, SD) are documented for in-service teachers only, as pre-service teachers are in training. Grade levels include Primary and Secondary school levels.

The eligibility requirements for participants encompass their voluntary commitment to engage in the study, their proficiency in language instruction, and their acquaintance with Intelligent Tutoring Systems (ITS). Pre-service teacher were required to be currently enrolled in a teacher training program, whereas in-service instructors must possess a minimum of one year of teaching experience. In addition, participants must have had prior knowledge of ITS, acquired either through formal training or practical implementation in their classrooms. This guaranteed that participants possess pertinent expertise and understanding to offer substantial perspectives on the research inquiries.

Participants' prior exposure to ITS tools and systems

In this study, participants had prior exposure to two distinct ITSs, tailored to meet the different needs and experience levels of pre-service and in-service teachers. Pre-service teachers learned *TutorMate*, while in-service teachers learned the *Cognitive Tutor Language Lab*. *TutorMate* is designed as an introductory ITS to support language education by developing fundamental skills. This system provides interactive modules for vocabulary, grammar, and reading comprehension, offering real-time feedback to guide pre-service teachers in managing basic student performance metrics. In contrast, in-service teachers learned to use the *Cognitive Tutor Language Lab*, an advanced ITS with personalized feedback tools, progress-tracking analytics, and data-driven instructional support suitable for experienced educators. This system emphasizes adaptive learning paths, enabling seasoned teachers to adjust instruction based on continuous student assessment. The training sessions for each group occurred in different settings and durations. Pre-service teachers learned to use *TutorMate* during their teacher education program at their university's language lab, which involved one semester of weekly two-hour sessions. The objectives of this training included familiarization with the *TutorMate* interface and navigation, understanding the system's feedback mechanisms to support language practice in vocabulary and grammar, and learning to interpret basic data analytics to identify student learning gaps and adapt instruction accordingly. For in-service teachers, training in the *Cognitive Tutor Language Lab* was integrated into a week-long professional development workshop held at regional training centers. This advanced training covered using system analytics for tracking student progress over time, customizing lesson content based on real-time data insights, and implementing differentiated instruction by adapting materials to students' performance data.

The content of the ITS training was tailored to the experience levels of each group. Pre-service teachers focused on building fundamental ITS skills with *TutorMate*, practicing how to interpret simple feedback and apply it in structured lesson plans. In-service teachers, conversely, learned to employ *Cognitive Tutor Language Lab*'s comprehensive analytics and adaptive feedback, providing them with more advanced control to tailor lessons and engage in nuanced instructional strategies that align with their classroom experience. By employing two distinct ITSs, this training ensured that both pre-service and in-service teachers could utilize ITS in ways that met their particular needs and experience levels.

Data collection

The data-gathering process for this study employs many ways to guarantee a thorough comprehension of the influence of Intelligent Tutoring Systems (ITS) on language teacher education. The main techniques for gathering data consist of surveys, classroom observations, and the examination of student performance statistics. Each approach is specifically developed to capture distinct facets of the study topics, offering a comprehensive perspective on the efficacy of ITS.

Surveys

Surveys has been conducted to collect data on instructors' experiences, perspectives, and attitudes about ITS. The survey questionnaires are specifically crafted to gather comprehensive data regarding teachers' experiences, perspectives, and attitudes toward Intelligent Tutoring Systems (ITS). The questionnaires are constructed using established measures from prior studies, including the Technology Acceptance Model (TAM) and the Unified Theory of Acceptance and Use of Technology (UTAUT). These models offer a conceptual structure for comprehending the aspects that affect the adoption and utilization of technology, guaranteeing that the survey collects pertinent and significant data. The questionnaires underwent pilot testing with a limited number of teachers to improve the items and verify that they were clear and understandable.

Classroom observations

The classroom observations provided qualitative insights that enhanced the quantitative findings from the survey data. We conducted structured observations across 20 classrooms, each for one full class period, focusing on the practical application of ITS by pre-service and in-service teachers. This structured observation was used to gauge ITS usage, teacher-student interactions, and the system's impact on teaching strategies and student engagement. Observational data indicated a significant difference between pre-service teachers, who mainly employed *TutorMate* for foundational skills, and in-service teachers, who used *Cognitive Tutor* for more advanced instructional customization. In-service teachers demonstrated higher levels of adaptive feedback and differentiated instruction, which were directly tied to student engagement improvements observed in the classroom settings.

Student performance data

Data on student performance data was gathered to assess the influence of ITS on learning outcomes. The data encompasses standardized test scores, grades, and other pertinent academic markers. The performance data was gathered for students who were taught by the participating in-service instructors, which offers a direct assessment of the usefulness of the ITS in improving student learning. The data was gathered during the specific academic year in which the study took place, ensuring that the performance measures accurately represent the influence of ITS throughout a substantial duration.

By utilizing these data collection methods, a thorough and diverse study of the research issues is guaranteed. The study utilizes triangulation of data from questionnaires, observations, and performance records to provide evidence on the influence of ITS on-language teacher education and student outcomes.

Data analysis

The Structural Equation Model was employed to assess the relationships among perceived usefulness, perceived ease of use, teaching efficacy, and student performance. The following null hypotheses (H0) were tested:

- **H0-1**: Perceived usefulness of ITS does not significantly influence teaching efficacy.
- **H0-2**: Perceived ease of use of ITS does not significantly influence teaching efficacy.
- **H0-3**: Teaching efficacy does not significantly influence student performance.
- **H0-4**: The perceived usefulness of ITS does not significantly influence student performance indirectly through teaching efficacy.
- **H0-5**: Perceived ease of use of ITS does not significantly influence student performance indirectly through teaching efficacy.

Descriptive statistics

The first step in data analysis involves computing descriptive statistics to provide a full picture of the collected data. As shown in Table 2:

Table 2. Descriptive statistics of participants.

Participant Group	Number of Participants	Average Age (Years)	Standard Deviation (Age)	Gender (Female)	Gender (Male)	Prior Exposure to ITS (%)
Pre-service Teachers	100	24.5	2.8	52	48	35
In-service Teachers	100	38.2	7.6	52	48	70

Table 3. Descriptive statistics of key variables.

Variable	*M*	*SD*	Measurement Scale
Perceived Usefulness	4.1	0.6	5-point Likert
Perceived Ease of Use	3.8	0.7	5-point Likert
Teaching Efficacy	4.2	0.5	5-point Likert
Student Performance	80.5	10.2	Percentage

M: Mean; SD: Standard Deviation.

The demographic characteristics of the 200 participants, comprising of 100 pre-service and 100 in-service instructors, are delineated. The average age of the pre-service teachers is 24.5 years, with a standard deviation of 2.8. On the other hand, the instructors present employed have an average age of 38.2 years, with a standard deviation of 7.6. The gender distribution is nearly balanced, with roughly 52% of individuals identifying as female and 48% identifying as male. Moreover, the level of familiarity with ITS varies. Specifically, 35% of pre-service teachers and 70% of in-service teachers have prior experience with ITS. Descriptive statistics offer a concise overview of the survey responses on instructors' perceptions of ITS in Table 3. The mean perceived usefulness score is 4.1 with a standard variation of 0.6, assessed using a 5-point Likert scale. This indicates a generally positive perspective toward ITS. Teachers regard the ITS to be relatively user-friendly, as indicated by the average score of 3.8 (with a standard deviation of 0.7) for perceived ease of use, as mentioned. These first findings provide the basis for conducting more sophisticated research to explore the underlying relationships among the variables.

Confirmatory factor analysis (CFA)

Confirmatory factor analysis (CFA) is used to assess the validity and reliability of the constructs measured by the survey instruments. This inquiry focuses on analyzing the perceived utility, perceived simplicity, and the impact of Intelligent Tutoring Systems (ITS) on instructional efficacy and student outcomes. According to the CFA model, items related to perceived utility and ease of use are assigned to their respective latent variables. The initial CFA model is estimated using the maximum likelihood estimation method. The appropriateness of the model is evaluated by analyzing important fit indices, such as the Comparative Fit Index (CFI), Tucker-Lewis Index (TLI), Root Mean Square Error of Approximation (RMSEA), and Standardized Root Mean Square Residual (SRMR), as shown in Table 4:

Table 4. Confirmatory factor analysis (CFA) results.

Construct	Cronbach's Alpha	CFI	TLI	RMSEA	SRMR	Factor Loadings (Range)
Perceived Usefulness	0.87	0.95	0.93	0.05	0.04	0.70–0.85
Perceived Ease of Use	0.84	0.95	0.93	0.05	0.04	0.68–0.82

CFI: Comparative Fit Index; TLI: Tucker-Lewis Index; RMSEA: Root Mean Square Error of Approximation; SRMR: Standardized Root Mean Square Residual. The factor loadings indicate the strength of the relationships between each construct and its associated items.

The findings demonstrate a strong level of congruence, as evidenced by the Comparative Fit Index (CFI) of 0.95, the Tucker-Lewis Index (TLI) of 0.93, the Root Mean Square Error of Approximation (RMSEA) of 0.05, and the Standardized Root Mean Square Residual (SRMR) of 0.04. The indices provide evidence that the measurement model accurately reflects the data. Each item exhibits factor loadings that are statistically significant ($p < .001$) and exceed the recommended criterion of 0.60, indicating a strong level of construct validity. The reliability of the variables is evaluated through the utilization of Cronbach's alpha, yielding values of 0.87 for perceived utility and 0.84 for perceived ease of use, indicating a substantial degree of internal consistency. The outcomes of the CFA establish a robust basis for the subsequent SEM analysis, guaranteeing the precision and uniformity of the measurement model.

Structural Equation Modeling (SEM)

Once the measurement model is confirmed, the study proceeds to evaluate the relationships between variables using SEM. It is used to analyze the direct and indirect impacts of ITS on language teacher education and student outcomes. The concept suggests that the way people perceive the usefulness and user-friendliness of Intelligent Tutoring Systems (ITS) has a beneficial effect on how successful teaching is, which in turn affects students' academic success. The SEM model is created and generated using the maximum likelihood estimation method. The path coefficients are examined to evaluate the magnitude and statistical significance of the associations. The model incorporates both direct channels (e.g., the link between perceived usefulness and teaching efficacy) and indirect pathways (e.g., the connection between perceived ease of use and student performance, which is influenced by teaching efficacy.

As shown in Table 5:

The results reveal significant direct effects of perceived usefulness ($\beta = 0.45$, $p < .001$) and perceived ease of use ($\beta = 0.32$, $p < .01$) on teaching efficacy. Teaching efficacy, in turn, significantly predicts student performance ($\beta = 0.50$, $p < .001$). The indirect effects of perceived usefulness and ease of use on student performance, mediated by teaching efficacy, are

Table 5. Structural Equation Modeling (SEM) Results.

Pathway	Path Coefficient (β)	Significance (*p*)
Perceived Usefulness → Teaching Efficacy	0.45	<.001
Perceived Ease of Use → Teaching Efficacy	0.32	<.01
Teaching Efficacy → Student Performance	0.5	<.001
Perceived Usefulness → Student Performance	0.22	<.01
Perceived Ease of Use → Student Performance	0.18	<0.05

All coefficients are standardized beta values. Significance levels indicate the probability of relationships between the variables.

Table 6. Model Fit Indices for SEM.

Fit Index	Value	Threshold for Good Fit
Comparative Fit Index (CFI)	0.96	> 0.90
Tucker-Lewis Index (TLI)	0.94	> 0.90
Root Mean Square Error of Approximation (RMSEA)	0.04	< 0.05
Standardized Root Mean Square Residual (SRMR)	0.03	< 0.05

also significant. These findings support the model and highlight the critical role of teaching efficacy as a mediator in the relationship between ITS and student outcomes.

Model fit indices

The model demonstrates a high degree of congruence with the data, as indicated by the following fit indices: Comparative Fit Index (CFI) = 0.96, Tucker-Lewis Index (TLI) = 0.94, Root Mean Square Error of Approximation (RMSEA) = 0.04, and Standardized Root Mean Square Residual (SRMR) = 0.03. The indices show that the relationships between the variables are accurately represented by the SEM. The model and the observed data exhibit a significant concurrence, as evidenced by the elevated values of CFI and TLI, both surpassing the 0.90 criterion. The model's suitability is further validated by the low values of RMSEA (Root Mean Square Error of Approximation) and SRMR (Standardized Root Mean Square Residual), both of which are less than 0.05. The fit indices, in conjunction with the significant path coefficients, provide compelling evidence that supports the connections and the overall model (Table 6).

Discussion

This study offers valuable insights into the integration of ITS in language teacher education and its impact on student achievement and instructional effectiveness. The notable discovery is the substantial impact of perceived usefulness and simplicity of usage on instructional effectiveness. This aligns with the Technology Adoption Model (TAM) created by Davis (1989), which emphasizes the importance of various perspectives in the acceptance and use of technology. While the primary quantitative analysis was conducted using SEM to assess relationships among perceived usefulness, perceived ease of use, teaching efficacy, and student performance, the observational data complemented these findings by providing qualitative validation of the SEM results. It indicated that in-service teachers, more familiar with ITS functionalities, employed the *Cognitive Tutor* for adaptive instruction and individualized feedback, improving student engagement and lesson differentiation. Pre-service teachers, trained with *TutorMate*, mainly used it for vocabulary and basic assessments, often facing a learning curve with ITS integration. This data underscores ITS's role in enhancing teaching efficacy, especially when educators are confident in the system's use, aligning with the positive attitudes reflected in average perceived usefulness scores ($M = 4.1$, SD = 0.6) and ease of use ratings ($M = 3.8$, SD = 0.7) from the survey results. This corroborates the findings of previous research conducted by Ertmer and Ottenbreit-Leftwich (2010), which showed that teachers' proficiency in utilizing technology can enhance their instructional approaches and foster greater student engagement.

Concerning our first research question, which sought to determine the principal determinants affecting the efficacy of Intelligent Tutoring Systems (ITS) in language teacher education, our results from the Structural Equation Modeling analysis provided additional clarity on these elements. The SEM findings indicated that both perceived usefulness and perceived ease of use significantly affected instructional efficacy, with perceived usefulness exerting a more substantial influence ($\beta = 0.45$, $p < .001$) than perceived ease of use ($\beta = 0.32$, $p < .01$). The observational data not only substantiates the SEM findings but also highlights practical applications of ITS. Observations demonstrated a distinct advantage for in-service teachers who utilized Cognitive Tutor's advanced feedback mechanisms. Pre-service teachers, still acclimating to ITS, showed a lower proficiency in adapting lessons through the technology, emphasizing the need for differentiated training. This aligns with our SEM results, where perceived usefulness ($\beta = 0.45$, $p < .001$) and teaching efficacy strongly predicted student outcomes. Observed student attentiveness was notably higher in classrooms where ITS supported adaptive learning and real-time feedback, further corroborating the SEM results. To optimize ITS integration, teacher training should tailor modules for varying experience levels, ensuring that both novice and experienced educators can leverage these technologies effectively for improved educational outcomes.

The link between perceived ease of use and teaching efficacy suggests that teachers are more likely to effectively integrate ITS into their teaching methods when they consider it to be user-friendly. For children, this might offer a more immersive and efficient learning setting. Hence, it is imperative to establish professional development initiatives that emphasize the tangible advantages of ITS and offer practical training to enhance their perceived worth and usability. These programs can enhance student achievement by enabling instructors to utilize these systems more efficiently and providing them with the resources to incorporate new technology into their lessons. Our study of the data indicated that the effectiveness of instruction significantly influences the outcomes of student learning. According to Locke's (1997) social cognitive theory, having a high belief in one's abilities to teach well can improve student progress. This is because educators with high levels of teaching efficacy can successfully meet the needs of their students, create positive learning environments, and utilize creative teaching methods. The results of the mediation study revealed a significant and robust association ($\beta = 0.50$, $p < .001$) between student performance and teachers' perceptions of ITS. Consequently, enhancing teachers' self-assurance can have a substantial impact on students' academic performance.

The SEM analysis further yielded substantial evidence in response to the third research question, which investigated the impact of ITS on student learning outcomes in language education. In particular, the SEM results demonstrated a substantial predictive relationship between student performance and teaching efficacy ($\beta = 0.50$, $p < .001$). The reliability of these findings is further substantiated by the high congruence of model fit indices (CFI = 0.96, TLI = 0.94, RMSEA = 0.04, SRMR = 0.03). These findings suggest that a robust foundation in ITS-supported teaching methodologies can result in improved academic performance among students by indirectly improving student learning outcomes through improved teaching efficacy.

The findings have significant ramifications for the training of language teachers. Given the favorable reception and good impact of ITS on student performance and instructional effectiveness, the inclusion of ITS training in teacher education programs has potential for positive outcomes. Including ITS in both pre-service and in-service teacher education programs is recommended to enhance educators' proficiency and confidence in utilizing them. Moreover, it is important that professional development programs prioritize the concrete advantages of ITS and provide practical guidance to enhance their perceived efficacy and user-friendliness. This approach can expedite the implementation of these systems while also guaranteeing that educators possess the essential resources to effectively utilize these technologies in order to enhance student achievements and their own instructional approaches.

This study provided some novel insights into the second research question, which studied the effects of ITS integration on the teaching practices of pre-service and in-service language teachers. A significant discovery was the varying effect of ITS on these two cohorts of educators. Pre-service instructors were still familiarizing themselves with these technologies, while in-service teachers demonstrated a greater dependence on Intelligent

Tutoring Systems, signifying its successful integration into regular instructional practices. This finding indicates a potential inadequacy in formal training for pre-service teachers, which may impede their ability to effectively utilize ITS. Consequently, by augmenting teacher training programs to incorporate increased practical experience with Intelligent Tutoring Systems, we may bridge this gap and ensure that both prospective and current educators are equally proficient in utilizing ITS to enhance education.

The utilization of SEM in this study provides a robust analytical framework for examining the complex relationships among educational efficacy, perceived usefulness, reported ease of use, and student achievement. By conducting a simultaneous examination of both direct and indirect influences, SEM provides a comprehensive knowledge of the mechanisms *via* which ITS influences educational results. The excellent fit indices of the SEM model (CFI = 0.96, TLI = 0.94, RMSEA = 0.04, SRMR = 0.03) provide strong evidence that the data strongly supports the predicted connections. This analytical method not only provides empirical evidence to support the theoretical framework but also offers guidelines for future research and practical application in integrating ITS into language teacher education.

The relationships among the key factors discussed here, Figure 1 presents a Structural Equation Model that visually represents the hypothesized and observed relationships between perceived usefulness, perceived ease of use, teaching efficacy, and student performance. This model integrates the findings discussed for each research question and provides a comprehensive overview of the interactions and impacts revealed in the study.

A unique aspect of this model is its integration of perspectives from both pre-service and in-service teachers, providing a comprehensive understanding of the impact of ITS across different stages of teacher development. This dual approach allows us to capture insights reflecting the varied experiences and needs of teachers at different points in their careers. Such integration is rarely observed in similar studies, making this model distinct in its ability to identify the nuances between different teacher cohorts.

The analysis shows that the perceived usefulness and ease of use of ITS are significant predictors of teaching efficacy. This finding aligns well with the Technology Acceptance Model, where perceived usefulness and ease of use are established determinants of technology adoption in educational settings. Furthermore, the findings highlight a higher level of dependency on ITS among in-service teachers compared to pre-service teachers. This suggests that in-service teachers may be more comfortable or reliant on ITS, potentially due to their greater familiarity with teaching needs. It also points to a possible gap in exposure or training for pre-service teachers, which might influence their readiness to effectively integrate ITS into their practice. Addressing this gap through enhanced formal training

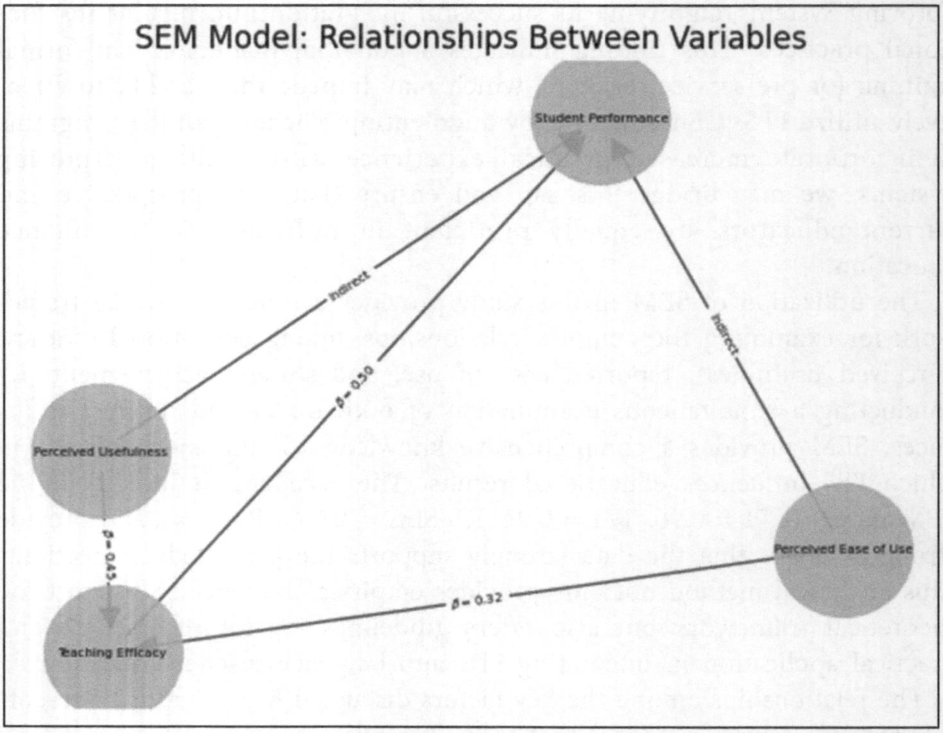

Figure 1. SEM Model Illustrating how ITS perceptions drive teaching efficacy and boost student performance.

programs, particularly hands-on experiences with ITS, could ensure more consistent and effective integration across both pre-service and in-service teachers.

Conclusion

This study provides valuable insights into the integration of Intelligent Tutoring Systems in language teacher education, highlighting its ability to improve teaching efficiency and foster student success. The findings of our study highlight the importance of users' perception of the utility and ease of use of ITS in order to effectively adopt and integrate them. These findings align with the Technology Acceptance Model. Moreover, the significance of teaching efficacy as a critical mediator is emphasized, emphasizing the need for professional development programs that enhance instructors' confidence and expertise in implementing ITS. Despite these promising findings, this analysis has several limitations. The sample size, albeit varied, may not effectively reflect all language teachers, therefore affecting the generalizability of the findings. Future investigations should aim to include a larger and more diverse sample in order to validate these findings in various educational contexts. Moreover, the study relied on self-reported data, which is vulnerable to biases such as social desirability and recall bias. A more comprehensive understanding of the consequences of ITS could be attained by incorporating additional data sources, such as longitudinal observations and student performance measurements across time. In addition, this study focused mainly on assessing the perceived usefulness and ease of use of the ITS, without thoroughly exploring other factors such as institutional support, technological infrastructure, and specific aspects of the system. Further research should investigate these issues to offer a holistic viewpoint on the barriers and enablers of integrating ITS.

In the future, there will be numerous avenues for additional research. An inquiry into the lasting effects of ITS on the accomplishments of instructors and learners would provide valuable insights into the sustained effectiveness of these technologies in educational settings. Moreover, doing an analysis of the specific attributes of ITS that have the most significant influence on the effectiveness of teaching and the academic performance of students could aid in the development of more streamlined systems tailored to the needs of language educators. Additional research should examine the influence of continuous professional growth and peer support networks on fostering a positive attitude toward Intelligent Tutoring Systems. This will ensure that educators remain engaged and proficient in their use of these tools.

Disclosure statement

No potential conflict of interest was reported by the author(s).

ORCID

Soumya Sankar Ghosh http://orcid.org/0000-0002-4469-4070

References

Anderson, J. R., Corbett, A. T., Koedinger, K. R., & Pelletier, R. (1995). Cognitive tutors: Lessons learned. *Journal of the Learning Sciences*, *4*(2), 167–207. https://doi.org/10.1207/s15327809jls0402_2

Black, W. C., Babin, B. J., & Anderson, R. E. (2010). *Multivariate data analysis: A global perspective*. Pearson.

Blake, R. J. (2013). *Brave new digital classroom: Technology and foreign language learning* Georgetown University Press.

Brown, T. A. (2015). *Confirmatory factor analysis for applied research*. Guilford publications.

Byrne, B. M. (2013). *Structural equation modeling with Mplus: Basic concepts, applications, and programming*. Routledge Press.

Chiu, T. L., Liou, H. C., & Yeh, Y. (2007). A study of web-based oral activities enhanced by automatic speech recognition for EFL college learning. *Computer Assisted Language Learning*, *20*(3), 209–233. https://doi.org/10.1080/09588220701489374

Darling-Hammond, L., Wei, R. C., Andree, A., Richardson, N., & Orphanos, S. (2009). Professional learning in the learning profession. Washington, DC: National Staff Development Council.

Davis, F. D. (1989). Perceived usefulness, perceived ease of use, and user acceptance of information technology. *MIS Quarterly*, *13*(3), 319–340. https://doi.org/10.2307/249008

Desimone, L. M. (2009). Improving impact studies of teachers' professional development: Toward better conceptualizations and measures. *Educational Researcher*, *38*(3), 181–199. https://doi.org/10.3102/0013189X08331140

Ertmer, P. A., & Ottenbreit-Leftwich, A. T. (2010). Teacher technology change: How knowledge, confidence, beliefs, and culture intersect. *Journal of Research on Technology in Education*, *42*(3), 255–284. https://doi.org/10.1080/15391523.2010.10782551

Freeman, D., & Johnson, K. E. (1998). Reconceptualizing the knowledge-base of language teacher education. *TESOL Quarterly*, *32*(3), 397–417. https://doi.org/10.2307/3588114

Graesser, A. C., Conley, M. W., & Olney, A. (2012). Intelligent tutoring systems In: K. R. Harris, S. Graham, T. Urdan, A. G. Bus, S. Major, & H. L. Swanson (Eds.), *APA educational psychology handbook, Vol. 3. Application to learning and teaching* (pp. 451–473). American Psychological Association.

Guernsey, L., & Levine, M. H. (2015). *Tap, click, read: Growing readers in a world of screens*. John Wiley & Sons.

Holland, V. M., Sams, M. R., & Kaplan, J. D. (2013). *Intelligent language tutors: Theory shaping technology*. Routledge.

Kline, R. B. (2023). *Principles and practice of structural equation modelling*. Guilford publications.

Koedinger, K. R., Anderson, J. R., Hadley, W. H., & Mark, M. A. (1997). Intelligent tutoring goes to school in the big city. *International Journal of Artificial Intelligence in Education*, *8*, 30–43.

Locke, E. A. (1997). Self-efficacy: The exercise of control. *Personnel Psychology*, *50*(3), 801.

Ma, W., Adesope, O. O., Nesbit, J. C., & Liu, Q. (2014). Intelligent tutoring systems and learning outcomes: A meta-analysis. *Journal of Educational Psychology*, *106*(4), 901–918. https://doi.org/10.1037/a0037123

Nakata, T. (2011). Computer-assisted second language vocabulary learning in a paired-associate paradigm: A critical investigation of flashcard software. *Computer Assisted Language Learning*, *24*(1), 17–38. https://doi.org/10.1080/09588221.2010.520675

Richards, J. C. (2008). Second language teacher education today. *RELC Journal*, *39*(2), 158–177. https://doi.org/10.1177/0033688208092182

Ritter, S., Anderson, J. R., Koedinger, K. R., & Corbett, A. (2007). Cognitive tutor: Applied research in mathematics education. *Psychonomic Bulletin & Review*, *14*(2), 249–255. https://doi.org/10.3758/bf03194060

Stark, D. R. (2016). *Equity starts early: How chiefs will build high-quality early education. A Policy Statement of the Council of Chief State School Officers*. Council of Chief State School Officers. https://files.eric.ed.gov/fulltext/ED580947.pdf

Stevenson, M., & Phakiti, A. (2014). The effects of computer-generated feedback on the quality of writing. *Assessing Writing*, *19*, 51–65. https://doi.org/10.1016/j.asw.2013.11.007

VanLehn, K. (2011). The relative effectiveness of human tutoring, intelligent tutoring systems, and other tutoring systems. *Educational Psychologist*, *46*(4), 197–221. https://doi.org/10.1080/00461520.2011.611369

VanLehn, K., Siler, S., Murray, C., Yamauchi, T., & Baggett, W. B. (2003). Human tutoring: Why do only some events cause learning. *Cognition and Instruction*, *21*(3), 209–249. https://doi.org/10.1207/S1532690XCI2103_01

Vescio, V., Ross, D., & Adams, A. (2008). A review of research on the impact of professional learning communities on teaching practice and student learning. *Teaching and Teacher Education*, *24*(1), 80–91. https://doi.org/10.1016/j.tate.2007.01.004

Wang, J., & Wang, X. (2019). *Structural equation modeling: Applications using Mplus*. John Wiley & Sons.

Warschauer, M., & Grimes, D. (2008). Automated writing assessment in the classroom. *Pedagogies: An International Journal*, *3*(1), 22–36. https://doi.org/10.1080/15544800701771580

Appendix A

This survey aims to capture language teachers' perspectives on Intelligent Tutoring Systems (ITS), specifically regarding their perceived usefulness, ease of use, teaching efficacy, and observed student performance.

Demographic information

1. Full Name: ______________________________
2. Participant Role:
   [] Pre-service Teacher
   [] In-service Teacher
3. Name of School/Institute (if In-service Teacher): ______________________________
4. Location of School/Institute (if In-service Teacher): ______________________________
5. State of Residence: ______________________________
6. Age: _______
7. Gender:
   [] Female
   [] Male
   [] Other
8. Years of Teaching Experience: _______
9. Highest Degree Completed:
   [] Bachelor's
   [] Master's
   [] Doctorate
10. Prior Exposure to ITS Tools:
    [] Yes
    [] No

Perceived usefulness of ITS

(Use a 5-point Likert scale: 1 = Strongly Disagree, 5 = Strongly Agree)

1. ITS helps me perform my teaching tasks more efficiently.
2. Using ITS increases my productivity in the classroom.
3. ITS enables me to provide more individualized instruction to students.
4. ITS allows me to monitor and adjust student progress more effectively.

5. I believe ITS enhances the overall quality of my teaching.
6. ITS assists me in creating a more engaging learning environment for students.
7. I find that ITS provides valuable insights for assessing student learning needs.

Perceived ease of use of ITS

(Use a 5-point Likert scale: 1 = Strongly Disagree, 5 = Strongly Agree)

1. It is easy to learn how to use ITS tools effectively.
2. The interface of ITS is user-friendly and accessible.
3. I can quickly navigate ITS functionalities without confusion.
4. Overall, I find ITS easy to use in classroom settings.
5. The time required to learn ITS does not interfere with my teaching responsibilities.
6. I feel supported in resolving any issues I encounter with ITS.
7. ITS provides clear guidance on how to incorporate it into lessons.

Teaching efficacy

(Use a 5-point Likert scale: 1 = Strongly Disagree, 5 = Strongly Agree)

1. I am confident in my ability to use ITS to enhance my teaching effectiveness.
2. ITS enables me to address diverse learning needs within my class.
3. I believe I can adapt my teaching approach based on insights provided by ITS.
4. I feel well-prepared to integrate ITS into my lesson plans.
5. I can effectively manage and guide students using ITS features.
6. I feel competent in customizing ITS content to suit my students' needs.
7. My teaching has become more targeted and purposeful with ITS.

Student performance

(Use a 5-point Likert scale: 1 = Strongly Disagree, 5 = Strongly Agree)

1. My students are more engaged in lessons that include ITS.
2. ITS has a positive impact on my students' comprehension and skill development.
3. ITS enables students to work more independently and confidently.
4. I have observed improvement in student test scores and grades with the use of ITS.
5. My students demonstrate greater motivation in using ITS compared to traditional methods.
6. Students interact more actively with content when using ITS.
7. ITS helps students retain and apply concepts more effectively over time.

Open-ended questions

1. Describe any challenges you have encountered when using ITS in the classroom.
2. In what ways has ITS influenced your approach to lesson planning and delivery?
3. Provide any specific examples of ITS impacting your students' learning experience positively or negatively.
4. What additional features or improvements would you like to see in ITS tools to support your teaching?

How does ITS compare with other teaching aids or strategies you have used?

The Integration of ChatGPT in English for Foreign Language Course: Elevating AI Writing Assistant Acceptance

Urai Salam

ABSTRACT

This study examines the integration of ChatGPT into English language learning by exploring students' experiences of using ChatGPT during the writing process. Adopting a convergent mixed-method design, the research involved students enrolled in the *ICT for ELT* course at a university in West Kalimantan, Indonesia, and applied the Technology Acceptance Model to explore the relationships among key variables. Ninety-five English as a Foreign Language (EFL) students participated in a four-week take-home assignment using a writing prompt provided by their lecturer. Qualitative data were collected through an open-ended questionnaire, which revealed that students' acceptance of ChatGPT was attributed to its user-friendly interface and ability to interact in their native language. Path analysis revealed that perceived ease of use positively influenced both perceived usefulness and attitude toward change, while perceived usefulness also positively affected attitude toward change. In turn, a positive attitude toward changes significantly impacted students' behavioral intentions to use ChatGPT. Integrating qualitative and quantitative findings, this study suggests that ChatGPT fostered a positive attitude toward technological change and encouraged students to adopt it more frequently. Notably, students primarily used ChatGPT as a writing aid rather than for generating complete essays, suggesting the potential for using ChatGPT under instructor supervision to diminish risks of dishonesty in academic writing.

Introduction

The importance of chatbot technology in language learning has grown with recent advancements in artificial intelligence (AI). Although this approach is relatively new, the use of chatbots to learn languages has received considerable attention in recent years. Several researchers (Guo et al., 2022; Kasneci et al., 2023) have attempted to integrate chatbot technology into language learning. Previous studies on the use of chatbots for language learning have demonstrated their effectiveness in enhancing language learning experiences. For example, chatbots can engage students in conversations (Yang et al., 2022) and provide them with immediate feedback (Kılıçkaya, 2020; Nagata et al., 2020), which can be helpful for language learners who need to practice their target language skills. Chatbots can also provide learners with additional practice and support in areas where they may struggle to handle unfamiliar vocabularies (Jeon, 2023; Qasem et al., 2023) and translation work (El Hefny et al., 2021).

Despite the fact that chatbot technology for language learning is becoming increasingly popular, it remains unclear how chatbots should be included in language education. This is partially due to the lack of research on the use of chatbots in language instruction and how they truly aid students in language acquisition. Other challenges include inadequate infrastructure and insufficient skills of instructors (Kasneci et al., 2023; Zhu et al., 2023) in using current technology that results in mixed reactions to its use, with some seeing it as a form of threatening academic integrity, while others view it as a potential tool for language learning exercises and a helpful writing assistant (Alharbi, 2023). These factors contribute to the overall uncertainty surrounding chatbot use in language education.

Chatbots have the potential to significantly enhance English language classrooms (Liu & Ma, 2024; Qasem et al., 2023); however, to realize their full potential, the impact of these technologies on the learning process must be studied rigorously. To examine the potential of chatbots as writing tools to enhance students' writing skills, educators need more deliberate implementation in their teaching scenarios. The current study aimed to investigate whether the deliberate use of ChatGPT influences students' perceptions of this technology and their actual usage for writing assistance. Previous studies have generally examined the role of ChatGPT in English as a Foreign Language (EFL) college learners in small samples with a focus on learner perceptions and writing skills (Hayashi & Sato, 2024; Yang & Li, 2024). There is limited research examining the application of ChatGPT integrated into courses, since most studies explore the use of ChatGPT for informal learning (Askarbekuly & Aničić, 2024; Liu & Ma, 2024; Yang & Li, 2024). Therefore, this study focuses on the use of ChatGPT in a writing course to ensure that results are not solely based on students' undefined use of ChatGPT or merely perceptions.

Technology acceptance model (TAM) to investigate ChatGPT

Previous studies have attempted to apply TAM to understand students' behavior in using ChatGPT. Saif et al. (2024) validated Technology Acceptance Model to understand ChatGPT use among university students in Pakistan. The TAM consists of technology acceptance, including perceived ease of use, perceived usefulness, feedback quality, assessment quality, subject norms, attitude toward use, and behavioral intention to use ChatGPT. Dahri et al. (2024) explored the TAM of the acceptance of ChatGPT for Metacognitive Self-Regulated Learning (MSRL). This study, involving personal competence, social influence, perceived AI trust, perceived AI usefulness, and perceived AI enjoyment to complete their TAM, shows a high acceptance of ChatGPT among university students in Malaysia. Barakat et al.'s (2024) studyinvolved social influence, technology readiness, anxiety, and perceived risk to understand Jordanian university educators use of ChatGPT.

The TAM predicts students' intention to use ChatGPT for education. Studies by Almogren et al. (2024) and Shaengchart (2023) show that perceived ease of use and perceived usefulness emerged as significant predictors of students' attitudes toward ChatGPT. Lai et al. (2023) found intrinsic motivation drives students' intention to use ChatGPT, with perceived usefulness being a strong predictor among university students in Hong Kong. Duong et al. (2023) investigated Vietnamese students and found effort expectancy positively affects performance expectancy, behavioral intention, and actual use of ChatGPT, with knowledge sharing as a moderator. Liu and Ma (2024) examined the TAM in informal English learning, revealing that students with high attitudes toward ChatGPT's usefulness have a higher behavioral intention to use it. Salloum et al. (2024) also found that students' behavioral intention predicts their use of ChatGPT in a translation class. Similarly, Shaengchart (2023) showed that perceived usefulness and ease of use components of the TAM significantly impact students' intentions to adopt ChatGPT technology. Considering the results of these previous studies, several hypotheses are proposed in this study:

- H1: Perceived ease of use positively affects perceived usefulness.
- H2: Perceived ease of use positively affects attitude toward change.
- H3: Perceived usefulness positively affects attitude toward change.
- H4: Attitude toward change positively affects behavioral intention

Experimental studies with ChatGPT

Several studies have investigated the use of ChatGPT to support students' English language learning. Xiao (2024) explored ChatGPT in a writing assistance role in a 10-week experiment on EFL learners in an English writing class. Using a comparison between the experimental and control groups, the study showed that students in the experimental group outperformed those in the control group in terms of content, structure, and language use. Tshai et al. (2024) used an experimental design to confirm that ChatGPT-assisted revised essays lead to considerably better results for EFL college English majors. In contrast, Niloy et al. (2024), conducted an experiment on students' creative writing in terms of presentation, accuracy, and elaboration in ten universities, and found that ChatGPT shows a negative effect on student creative writing.

Hayashi and Sato (2024) conducted a 4-week experiment and found that daily 10-minute use of ChatGPT improves students' English proficiency and reduces second language anxiety. Shaikh et al. (2023) used a questionnaire-based approach to explore respondents' opinions on ChatGPT after English tasks like conversation, writing, grammar, and vocabulary, highlighting its effectiveness in formal English learning. A one-case shot pre-experimental design conducted by Punar Özçelik and Yangın Ekşi (2024) added that the use of ChatGPT supports students' knowledge of formal registers during academic writing but is unnecessary for informal learning. Songsiengchai et al. (2023) included preservice teachers in Thailand in an experiment with ChatGPT, noting its personalized and engaging nature based on participant self-reports. Wang and Feng (2023) conducted a 4-week experiment at a Chinese university, revealing that students using ChatGPT for reading assistance increased their reading comprehension rate by over 86%. However, across previous studies there is a lack of research examining how ChatGPT is actually used.

Method

Design

This study aims to examine the benefits of using ChatGPT in an educational context by examining students' perceptions and experiences of using ChatGPT during the writing process. To accomplish this objective, a convergent mixed-method design integrating both quantitative and qualitative data collection techniques was used. A convergent mixed-method design entails simultaneous collection and analysis of quantitative and qualitative data in a single phase (Creswell & Clark, 2018). This study employed convergent mixed-method to maintain equal importance for both qualitative and quantitative findings. Both analyses were run independently but complemented each other. The qualitative results provide deep contextual insights, while the quantitative results show statistical patterns that support the findings. These two distinct types of data are expected to provide a more profound understanding and broader perspective of the phenomenon under investigation.

Instruments

To gather quantitative data, the study employed Davis (1989) TAM questionnaire with a 5-point Likert scale to assess students' perception of

ChatGPT use for writing. It includes perceived usefulness (PU) and perceived ease of use (PEU), both of which influence attitude toward the usage of ChatGPT (ATU) and subsequently affect behavioral intentions (BI). In essence, instrument considers how the user-friendliness and usefulness of ChatGPT shape learners' attitude toward the tool and influence their willingness to incorporate it into their learning process. The questionnaire comprised ten adapted items organized into four constructs: Perceived Usefulness (PU), Perceived Ease of Use (PEU), Attitude Toward ChatGPT (ATC), and Behavioral Intention (BI) (see Appendix A).

To inquire more deeply into the students' experiences with ChatGPT, qualitative data were collected through open-ended questions allowing for a richer exploration of their experiences and thoughts in using ChatGPT by answering the following three questions. The first open-ended question is "*according to your experience, in what ways did ChatGPT assist you in writing?*" This question aims to explore the specific ways in which ChatGPT has been helpful in the writing process. The second one is "*what convenience do you gain from using ChatGPT in learning writing*?" This question highlights the efficiency and effectiveness of using ChatGPT as a learning tool. The third question is "*would you recommend the use of ChatGPT to friends and others?" Why?*" This question explored users' confidence and willingness to recommend ChatGPT to others and the reasons behind their recommendations.

Procedure and participants

The participants were first semester EFL under graduate students enrolled in the *ICT for ELT* course at the English Education Department of a university in West Kalimantan, Indonesia. After gaining ethical approval from the faculty, the study proceeded in three phases (See Figure 2). The questionnaire was administered anonymously online using *Google Form* both before and after intervention (phases 1 and 3). In Phase 1, 158 students participated in a pre-intervention survey. The survey revealed that 95 respondents had prior experience using ChatGPT at varying levels of proficiency; consequently, they were invited to complete the Technology Acceptance Model (TAM) questionnaire. Meanwhile, 63 respondents indicated that they were unfamiliar with ChatGPT and therefore did not participate in the subsequent process. In Phase 2, to ensure that students' perceptions were based on their true experiences rather than mere opinions, 95 students engaged in writing activities involving ChatGPT (See Figure 1).

As the course lecturer, I offered students a 4-week take-home assignment to write a 300-word essay in English on the topic "Technology in Language Education." While English served as the language of instruction, students were allowed to draft in Indonesian to express their ideas more fluently.

Writing Prompt: ChatGPT for Academic Writing

Instructions:

- Write an essay of approximately 300 words describing how technology is used in language education.
- You may write in Indonesian to help you write faster and more fluently.
- Work withChatGPT to improve the quality of your essay. For example, ask for feedback on clarity and coherence, translation, and other possibilities.
- You have four weeks to practice using ChatGPT. Share your prompts with your friends to get the most help from ChatGPT.
- Please save copies of your final essay.
- Keep a record of all the ChatGPT prompts you use while working on your writing.

Figure 1. Writing prompt for the 4-week take-home assignment.

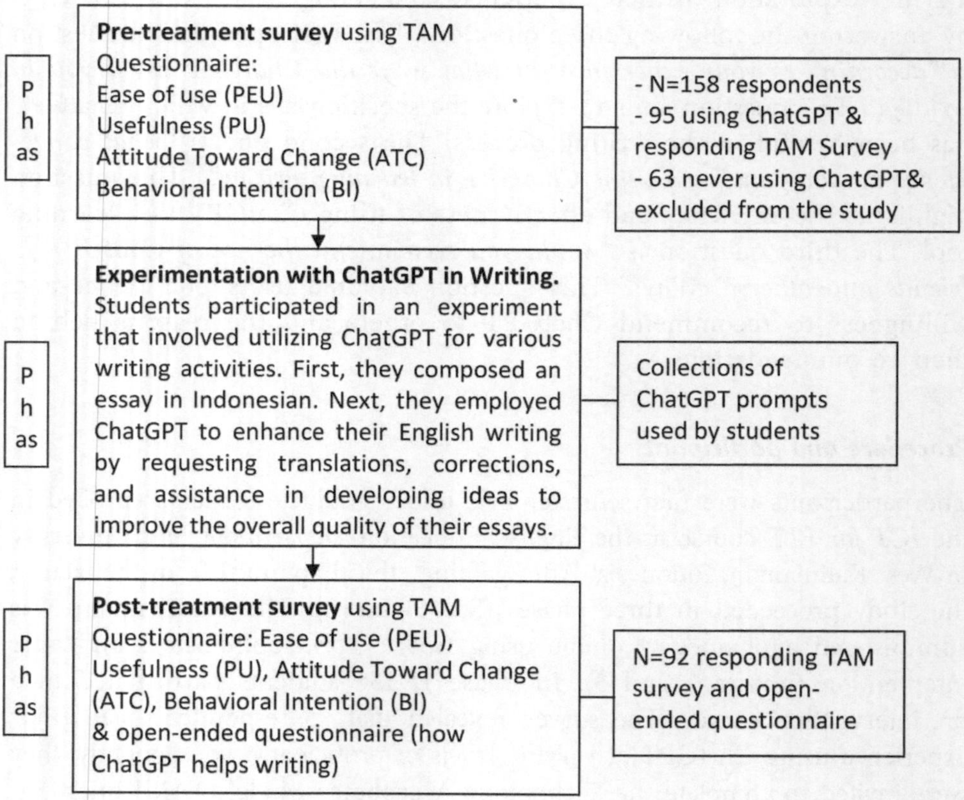

Figure 2. Research procedure.

Since the students were EFL learners who mainly communicated in Indonesian, drafting in their native language helped them avoid language barriers and focus on creativity. Once students had completed their drafts, they were required to utilize ChatGPT to refine and enhance their writing. This involved tasks such as translating into English, editing for clarity, improving the overall quality of their ideas, and correcting English structures. This encouraged the use of the ChatGPT as a tool to elevate their writing. The primary aim of this exercise was to provide students with hands-on experience using ChatGPT as a writing aid, thereby enabling them to comprehend both its challenges and benefits. The writing instructions given to students are presented in Figure 1.

In Phase 3, the respondents ($N=95$) were required to complete the same TAM questionnaires and open-ended ones. For more detailed explanation, the procedure of the study is presented in Figure 2.

Thematic analysis of students' responses

The open-ended questionnaire responses were examined using thematic analysis as outlined by Kiger and Varpio (2020). The analysis consisted of six iterative steps: (1) becoming familiar with the data, (2) generating initial codes based on relevant comments, (3) organizing the codes into preliminary thematic clusters, (4) reviewing the data and refining the themes to ensure the representativeness of all responses, (5) assigning names to each theme, and (6) drafting the final report. These steps were not strictly sequential and were revisited as needed.

Results

In this study, presenting the qualitative findings first allowed me to explore participants' perspectives as well as contextual factors, thus providing a more complete insight into the phenomenon being analyzed. These understanding offer a foundation for interpreting the statistical relationships identified in the quantitative analysis. By combining theme analysis and path analysis, this study not only provides qualitative context that deepens understanding of the mechanisms of relationships between variables, but also explains the quantitative relationships between them.

The qualitative findings were organized into four sections following the TAM structure: (1) perceived ease of use, (2) perceived usefulness, (3) attitude toward change, and (4) behavioral intention. Data from closed-ended questionnaires are reported using descriptive statistics, while findings from open-ended questionnaires are presented through thematic analysis, including codes and representative quotes to illustrate the identified themes.

Perceived ease of use (PEU)

The survey explored the theme of Ease of Use in relation to ChatGPT. The questionnaire consisted of three questions (PEU1, PEU2, and PEU3) related to the ease of understanding and usability of ChatGPT as in Table 1. The first question indicated that, on average, respondents found ChatGPT to be clear and understandable. Similarly, for the second question, PEU2 suggested that most respondents found it easy to use ChatGPT to accomplish their

Table 1. Descriptive statistics of the ease-of-use variable.

Theme	Questionnaire	Mean	SD
Ease of Use	PEU1. ChatGPT is clear and understandable.	4.31	.95
	PEU2. I find it easy to use ChatGPT to do what I want it to do	4.26	.99
	PEU3. I find ChatGPT easy to use	4.55	.85

Table 2. Sub-theme, codes, and quotes related to ease of use of ChatGPT.

No	Sub-theme	Code	Quote
1	Ease of access and use	Easy to use, easy to access, apply	"ChatGPT is very easy to use and provides quick answers." "I can easily access the information I need through ChatGPT."
2	Use of multi-language	Various languages	"ChatGPT can understand and respond in multiple languages, making it very flexible." "With ChatGPT, I can type sentences in multiple languages and get appropriate responses."
3	Ease of Finding Information	Get information, easily and quickly	"ChatGPT helps me get the necessary information easily and quickly."

desired tasks. However, both questions indicate some variability in opinions. Finally, for the third question, PEU3 indicated that most respondents perceived ChatGPT as easy to use, with a higher level of agreement among the participants compared to the previous two questions. Overall, the survey data suggest that ChatGPT is generally considered clear, understandable, and easy to use by most respondents.

The themes for the ease of use of ChatGPT as presented in Table 2 included ease of access and use, multilanguage use, and ease of finding information. Students found ChatGPT advantageous because it was user-friendly and intuitive. Anyone from any background can use it because it is not limited to a specific language. Since English is a foreign language in Indonesia, the ability of ChatGPT to understand Bahasa Indonesia attracts students to use it. Students also expressed their admiration for the rapid responses ChatGPT may provide. Students also noted that ChatGPT understood the simple prompts written by the students.

Perceived usefulness (PU)

Table 3 indicates that, on average, respondents perceived ChatGPT as having a positive impact on their English writing development (PU1). Similarly, for the second question (PU2), most respondents reported that ChatGPT enhanced their productivity in English writing practice, although the average level of agreement was slightly lower than that of the previous question. Lastly, for the third question, PU3, most respondents regarded ChatGPT as an excellent tool for improving the quality of their English writing. Although there is some variability in opinions, the overall trend suggests that ChatGPT has the potential to be a valuable tool for individuals seeking to enhance their English writing ability.

Table 3. Descriptive statistics of the perceived usefulness variable.

Theme	Questionnaire	Mean	SD
Perceived Usefulness	PU1. Using ChatGPT improves my learning of English Writing	4.20	.86
	PU2. Using ChatGPT increase my productivity in English writing practice	3.88	.93
	PU3. ChatGPT is excellent tool to improve the quality of my English writing.	4.20	.87

The students' answers to the open-ended questionnaire indicated the extent to which the ChatGPT scaffolded their writing tasks. They indicated that ChatGPT improved their writing performance and productivity when it came to generating ideas, expanding, and enriching their writing content, paraphrasing, and recasting sentences, providing writing feedback and suggestions, improving structure and flow, adding, and subtracting the length of words, and improving efficiency as presented in Table 4.

The results also indicated that ChatGPT helped students in the initial stage of writing by discovering topics for writing and generating ideas for the topic. Students used ChatGPT to brainstorm their ideas and simplify them to produce simpler ideas to be expanded into paragraphs. Once they developed the topics for each paragraph, they used ChatGPT to provide more ideas, such as examples to support the topics. They also used ChatGPT to summarize the papers they cited. Students used ChatGPT to paraphrase their ideas before putting them on their writing assignments. They noted that this helped them avoid plagiarism. In paraphrasing their ideas, the students asked ChatGPT to paraphrase the sentence by looking for synonyms and antonyms of words. They also used ChatGPT to check whether their vocabulary selection was appropriate for terms and registers.

ChatGPT was used to check whether students' writings were organized and flowed smoothly by evaluating the storyline and rearranging their sentences. ChatGPT helped students lengthen and shorten their writing tasks without changing the content of their paragraphs. Since the writing tasks instructed students to write an essay in 300 words, they employed ChatGPT to ensure that all their ideas in writing were covered in the word limit. After ensuring that they finished their writing, the students used ChatGPT again to review overall writing. They expressed their admiration for ChatGPT because it saved time.

Attitude toward change (ATC)

On average theATC1 question indicated that, in general, respondents found ChatGPT very interesting as in Table 5. Meanwhile, ATC2 showed that respondents moderately expected their learning activities to involve the use of ChatGPT. The answers indicated mixed opinions regarding the items in this variable.

Attitudes toward change indicate how students react to change. In this case, the responses shown in Table 6 indicated that they adapted to use

Table 4. Sub-theme, codes, and quotes related to perceived usefulness of ChatGPT.

No	Theme	Sub-theme	Code	Quote
1	Idea Generation	Idea Generation and Brainstorming	• Topic discovery • Idea generation for writing • Idea streamlining • Creativity catalyst • Scope broadening • Concept simplification	"ChatGPT really helped me with my writing. It helped me find ideas and develop my text into one solid idea." "ChatGPT gives me a new perspective on a discussion, which I can use to improve my writing."
2		Content Expansion and Enrichment	• New ideas and perspectives • Exemplification • Summarization • Alternative viewpoints • Argument Development and Analysis	"ChatGPT helps me add more examples or more detailed explanations in the topics I write about." "... as well as explanations that if I were to look up on the Internet, (it) would take longer than asking ChatGPT." "ChatGPT gave me some ideas for writing that I might not have thought of before." "ChatGPT provides strong arguments and in-depth analysis for certain topics."
3	Styling and Paraphrasing	Paraphrasing and Recasting Sentences	• Paraphrasing	"Another example related to writing is when I need to write polite sentences, I can ask ChatGPT to provide feedback and corrections" "ChatGPT is very helpful to my writing, especially for paraphrasing"
4		Writing Feedback and Suggestion	• Grammar improvement, punctuation, and vocabulary, Selection of appropriate vocabulary • Suggestion, improvement, feedback, writing revision, Mistake rectification • Identification of synonyms and antonyms	"ChatGPT is very helpful (to my writing) especially paraphrasing. "... in making words without convoluted" "ChatGPT was very helpful in providing suggestions and improvements to my paper." "ChatGPT provided useful feedback for my revision."
5	Content	Structure and Flow	• Contribution to the development of smoother and more natural texts, Essay structuring • Idea rearrangement for fluent flow	"ChatGPT helps me create more structured and organized writing." "I often use ChatGPT to revise my writing ..., and make sure my storyline is logical."
6		Addition and Subtraction of Content	• Lengthen, abbreviate, add material, relevant information, Text length adjustment	"ChatGPT can lengthen or shorten a text according to my needs." "Help me develop ideas, correct grammar, punctuation, and vocabulary, shorten or lengthen a text, and provide feedback on my writing."
7		Writing evaluation	• Manuscript review	"ChatGPT gives better results for my writing, and inform me what to do to make my writing better."
8	Efficiency	Time and Effort Savings	• Save time, faster, efficient	"ChatGPT saves my time" "With ChatGPT, I can complete tasks more quickly and efficiently."

Table 5. Descriptive statistics of the attitude toward change variable.

Theme	Questionnaire	Mean	SD
Attitude Toward Change	ATC1. ChatGPT is interesting	4.60	.82
	ATC2. I hope my learning activity is related to the use of ChatGPT	3.99	.97

ChatGPT in their writing tasks. A person may seek support and contribute to the change process, or resist and try to avoid change. If students think that ChatGPT causes detrimental effects, they will stop using it, and vice

Table 6. Sub-theme, codes, and quotes related to attitude toward change.

No	Sub-theme	Code	Quote
1	User Satisfaction and Acceptance	User Recommendation	"Yes, I will recommend it to my other friends, so that they know that there is advanced technology that can do anything just by chatting." "I have even recommended this both to my friends because I think the use of this bot is not only limited in the field of education but in any field such as art, language, history, technology, even small problems in our daily life."
2	Consistent Usage	General Helpfulness	"... ChatGPT is very helpful to me not only in Writing subjects, but also in almost all of my subjects. ChatGPT helps me find ideas, concepts, material descriptions, examples, and even create complete texts for the ideas I want, correct errors, and give advice on my writing." "ChatGPT is very helpful to create a story with the desired genre. Just type 'write a horror story', and ChatGPT will immediately provide text input."

Table 7. Descriptive statistics of the behavioral intention variable.

Theme	Questionnaire	Mean	SD
Behavioral Intention	BI1. I will use ChatGPT in the future.	4.27	.84
	BI2. I plan to use ChatGPT often	3.93	.94

Table 8. Sub-theme, codes, and quotes related to behavioral intention of using ChatGPT.

No	Sub-theme	Code	Quote
1	Behavioral Intention	I will recommend, I will use	"Yes, I will definitely recommend ChatGPT to other students" "Yes, I would recommend the use of ChatGPT to my friends." "I will use ChatGPT."

versa. The students' answers indicated their satisfaction with the use of ChatGPT to complete their writing tasks. They mentioned the advantages of the ChatGPT and recommended it to their friends. This shows that not only do they accept the change, but they also invite others to experience the same change since they eventually obtain advantages. Students' answers also indicated consistent use of ChatGPT, not only in the writing course, as they benefited from ChatGPT in completing their tasks. This indicates that students were ready for a change in which AI was integrated into courses.

Behavioral intention (BI)

The mean of the responses to the first question (BI1) shows that in general, respondents agree to use ChatGPT in the future (Table 7). Item BI2 shows slightly lower level of agreement than BI1. This indicates a greater variation in plans to frequently use ChatGPT among respondents.

The students' responses as in Table 8 indicated the extent to which a person plans or intends to carry out a particular behavior in the future. Someone with high behavioral intention shows a strong commitment to carrying out certain actions. Identifying and improving behavioral

Table 9. Sub-theme, codes, and quotes related to additional themes found in the study.

No	Sub-theme	Code	Quote
1	Skepticism and Criticism	I will recommend, I will use	"To be honest, ... using ChatGPT is cheating and (education) will end up with no competition." "Honestly no, because it will make people lazy to think and ChatGPT will be difficult to access if many people use it." I don't really recommend using ChatGPT because it reduces brain capacity to think independently as it relies heavily on ChatGPT. It's fine to use ChatGPT but don't rely on it given the information provided aren't necessarily true."
2	Conditional suggestion		"I would recommend using ChatGPT to friends and other students provided the person is someone with integrity and credibility. ChatGPT can be a positive or negative thing depending on the individual." "I recommend ChatGPT to some of my friends, but not to others. I recommend ChatGPT to my friends who I think can filter information, use it as needed or in other words do not depend entirely on ChatGPT, and can use it wisely."

intentions can be an important step in integrating AI into education. The responses showed students intention to recommend ChatGPT to others.

Additional themes

Additional themes emerged, offering interesting findings beyond those listed in previous sections. The themes presented in Table 9 included skepticism and criticism, as well as conditional suggestions. Some students criticize the integration of ChatGPT in writing courses since they think that only providing prompts and asking ChatGPT to finish writing is cheating. They were afraid that ChatGPT would make people lazy and lose their critical thinking. Some of them thought that not all information provided by ChatGPT was true, and that students should not rely solely on ChatGPT. This applies to the context in which students overly depend on ChatGPT to complete their writing.

Some students also expressed concerns that ChatGPT can be harmful when used without ethical integrity by a student. They believed that ChatGPT could only be used for writing assistance if students understood the advantages and disadvantages of its use. Students should understand the ethical considerations of using ChatGPT in writing courses. Therefore, some students said that they would recommend the use of ChatGPT to their friends with responsibility, integrity, and literacy.

The qualitative data analysis offered insights into students' experiences with ChatGPT, highlighting its ease of use, usefulness in improving writing skills, attitudes toward new technologies, future use intentions, and concerns or criticisms about its role in academic writing. The next step involved hypothesis testing to explore the benefits of ChatGPT in supporting student writing. The combined qualitative and quantitative analysis demonstrated that the advantages of ChatGPT were evident not only through participants' perceptions and experiences but also through quantitative evidence from path analysis. The quantitative analysis began with a classical assumption test and continued with path analysis.

Hypothesis testing on survey response items

Classical assumption test

The classical assumption test was conducted before the hypothesis testing. This included normality, heteroscedasticity, and multicollinearity tests. The classical assumption test ensures the model produces accurate and reliable parameter estimates. The normality of the residual was tested using the normal P-P plot graph, which indicates that the data distribution points are near the reference diagonal line, suggesting that the assumption is met. The heteroscedasticity test determines the distribution of the data to avoid extreme values. The results using the ZPRED and SRESID scatterplot graphs show that the plot points do not form a certain pattern; therefore, the assumption is met. The multicollinearity test shows no high correlation between independent variables, as all VIF values are below 10, confirming that the assumption is met.

Path test

The results of path test are presented in Table 10. The effect of PEU on PU yielded a path coefficient of .305 with a significance value (p) of .003. Since the p-value is less than .05, it indicates a significant positive relationship, meaning that the higher the PEU, the higher the PU. e1 is the error in the first equation. The coefficient of determination obtained a value of .093, indicating that the effect on perceived usefulness can be explained by 9.3% by perceived ease of use. The path equation is as follows:

$$PU = .305PEU + e1$$

The effect of PEU on ATC shows a path coefficient of .340 with a significance value (p) of .001. This indicates that the higher PEU, the higher the ATC. The path coefficient obtained was .283 with a significance value (p) of .004 suggesting a significant positive effect of PU on ATC.

Table 10. Path test results.

Variable	Path coefficient	t	p	Description
PEU → PU	.305	3.087	.003	Significant
R Square = .093				
PEU → ATC	.340	3.601	.001	Significant
PU → ATC	.283	2.993	.004	Significant
R Square = .255				
ATC → BI	.448	4.831	.000	Significant
R Square = .201				

Thus, the higher the PU, the higher the ATC. e2 is the error in the second equation. The coefficient of determination was .255, which indicates that the effect on ATC can be explained by 25.5% by PEU and PU. The path equation formed is:

$$ATC = .340\,PEU + .283\,PU + e2$$

The effect of ATC on BI shows a path coefficient of .448 with a significance value (p) of .000. The higher the ATC, the higher the BI, where e3 is the error in the third equation. The coefficient of determination is .201, indicating that the effect on BI can be explained by 20.1% by ATC.

$$BI = .305\,ATC + e3$$

Based on the results of the tests, the path diagram is illustrated in Figure 3.

In the context of path analysis, Q^2 refers to Predictive Relevance. It is used to evaluate how well the built model can predict endogenous variables (variables explained by the model). Q^2 measures the model's ability to predict the variation of relevant data for endogenous variables based on the predicted value of the model. In measuring the overall model, Q^2 can be calculated using the following formula:

$$Q^2 = 1 - (1 - R_1^2)(1 - R_2^2)(1 - R_3^2)$$
$$Q^2 = 1 - (1 - .093)(1 - .255)(1 - .201)$$
$$Q^2 = 1 - (.907 \times .745 \times .799)$$
$$Q^2 = 1 - .540$$
$$Q^2 = .460$$

A Q^2 value greater than .35 indicates that the model can predict endogenous variables well and has strong predictive ability. This model can describe the relationship between variables and has high relevance in predicting changes that occur in endogenous variables.

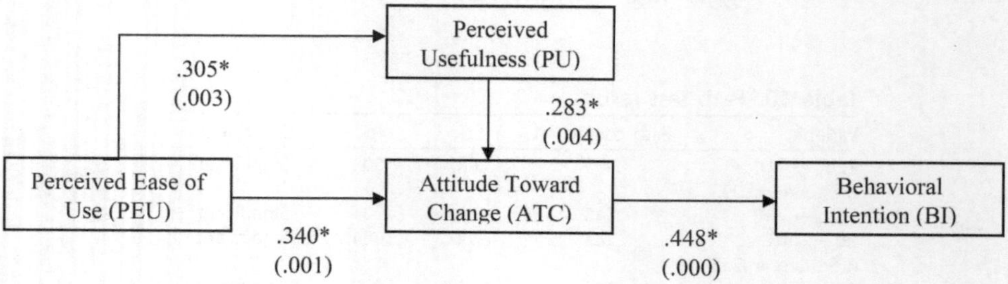

Figure 3. The path diagram of the study.

Table 10 shows the results of hypothesis testing. The effect of perceived ease of use on perceived usefulness obtained a t-value of 3.087 ($t > 1.960$) and a significance value of .003 ($p < .05$), indicating a significant influence, thus confirming Hypothesis 1. The effect of perceived ease of use on attitude toward change obtained a t-value of 3.601 ($t > 1.960$) and a significance value of .001 ($p < .05$), suggesting a significant influence. This indicates that Hypothesis 2 is accepted. The effect of perceived usefulness on attitude toward change showed a t-value of 2.993 ($t > 1.960$) and significance value of .004 ($p < .05$). Thus, perceived usefulness has a significant effect on attitudes toward change. Hypothesis 3 is proven to be correct. The effect between attitude toward change and attitude toward change obtained a t value of 4.831 ($t > 1.960$) and a significance value of .000 ($p < .05$), indicating a significant effect of attitude toward change on behavioral intention. Thus, Hypothesis 4 is accepted.

The combination of qualitative and quantitative findings provides a clear understanding of how ChatGPT is adopted for writing. The quantitative analysis confirms the relationships between ease of use, usefulness, attitudes, and intentions, offering statistical evidence for these connections. Meanwhile, the qualitative data explain the personal experiences behind these relationships, giving detailed insights into how participants interact with ChatGPT. The qualitative findings also highlight the benefits of using ChatGPT for writing, which match the patterns found in the quantitative analysis. Together, these results offer a complete and well-rounded view of ChatGPT adoption for writing.

Discussion

This study experimented the use of ChatGPT in the writing course. The actual use of ChatGPT in this study ensured that the responses generated by participants were not solely based on students' perceptions and undefined use of ChatGPT. In this study, the combination of qualitative and quantitative findings confirms that students benefit from the ease of use and usefulness of ChatGPT in supporting their academic writing. ChatGPT is an all-in-one AI with multiple functions, making it popular among students for assisting with writing. This finding is reinforced by the results of path analysis, which enhanced the understanding that the benefits students experienced motivated them to continue using ChatGPT for future coursework.

Our findings indicate that students view ChatGPT as a user-friendly chatbot that facilitates their work. Its friendly interface is easily accessible to language learners (Shaikh et al., 2023). It offers an understandable interface for students to put their questions and navigate its functions (Hasanein & Sobaih, 2023). Its rapid feedback, immediate explanation, and personalized learning add to learning efficiency (Hasanein & Sobaih, 2023; Kılıçkaya, 2020; Nagata et al., 2020; Xiao & Zhi, 2023). Respondents also felt that it saved time because ChatGPT can explain complicated or confusing concepts (Hasanein & Sobaih, 2023).

Students tend to be more accepting of change if they perceive the tangible benefits derived from new technology. Prior literature indicates that students who used AI for learning showed improved language skills (Songsiengchai et al., 2023). ChatGPT helps students perform academic tasks (Hasanein & Sobaih, 2023). It is often used for content creation and feedback (Yang & Li, 2024). ChatGPT also provides explanations and examples (Hasanein & Sobaih, 2023; Punar Özçelik & Yangın Ekşi, 2024) to help students outline their writing. Students often use it as a paraphrasing tool to avoid plagiarism. It can also summarize papers or help with data analysis (Hasanein & Sobaih, 2023). Students and teachers list language editing and proofreading equally as one of the main reasons for using ChatGPT in the classroom (Hasanein & Sobaih, 2023). ChatGPT provided corrections and suggestions such as grammar, punctuation, and sentence structure for professional wiring (Punar Özçelik & Yangın Ekşi, 2024). ChatGPT revises writing errors and ensures coherence and cohesiveness. It helps students convey ideas by assisting them in arranging sentences for coherence (Baskara & Mukarto, 2023; Hasanein & Sobaih, 2023). Despite assisting students with considerably lower-order language skills, such as syntax and grammar (Xiao & Zhi, 2023), ChatGPT can generate synonyms and antonyms along with their explanation for a greater variety of words (Qasem et al., 2023). It helps students find formal language appropriate to the context of their writing (Punar Özçelik & Yangın Ekşi, 2024). This suggests that ChatGPT is a potential resource for formal English language learning (Shaikh et al., 2023).

The incorporation of chatbots into courses may cause resistance in educational context (Zhu et al., 2023). ChatGPT may provide inaccurate, biased, and fabricated information (Fui-Hoon Nah et al., 2023; Nugroho et al., 2024). This research indicates that some students show discretion in using AI, including recommending it to others, due to the risks of AI-assisted cheating (Zhu et al., 2023). The resistance observed in this study highlights the importance of training on the use of AI in education to ensure that students are aware of its advantages and consequences. Students' perceptions may differ if they receive systematic training or guidance rather than exploring things independently (Xiao & Zhi, 2023). Training is essential to raise awareness of the potential strengths and weaknesses of ChatGPT (García-Alonso et al., 2024). In a related context, students' awareness is also demonstrated by participants in Sulissusiawan and Salam's study, where a student stated, "'Don't trust us … If we don't have a guideline, we don't know where to go…'" (Sulissusiawan & Salam, 2017, p. 47). Training is crucial because ChatGPT contributes less to or even restricts the development of language competence if students use it only as a ghostwriter to complete the tasks (Xiao & Zhi, 2023). Rather than prohibiting the use of these tools in the classroom or discouraging their use in writing assignments without monitoring or control, educators may need to investigate ways to incorporate them into the classroom and provide appropriate guidance. Additionally, students should be informed about plagiarism-detecting tools to mitigate potential misuse of the technology (Phuong, 2024). Human-teacher interactivity is still required in AI-assisted learning (Du & Alm, 2024).

Zhu et al. (2023) argued that ChatGPT offers limited capabilities to facilitate critical thinking and in-depth understanding. In contrast,Xiao and Zhi (2023) contend that while offering less assistance for sophisticated language skills, including writing logical and authentic essays, ChatGPT enhances critical thinking skills, such as when students modify prompts or ting the quality of ideas and outputs generated by ChatGPT. It can produce fluent and coherent text, but may have challenges understanding abstract or more complex ideas (Baskara & Mukarto, 2023).

Regardless of how language educators view the use of chatbots to complete writing tasks, it may be time to adopt a more pragmatic approach and embrace this issue as an unavoidable reality that must be addressed. Hence, ChatGPT should be integrated into instructional practices (Shaikh et al., 2023). Integrating chatbots in writing courses will educate students on how to use AI mindfully (Punar Özçelik & Yangın Ekşi, 2024). Clear guidelines and pedagogical approaches should be established emphasizing fact-checking strategies and critical thinking to mitigate ethical concerns regarding the use of AI in language learning (Hasanein & Sobaih, 2023; Kasneci et al., 2023). Overall, as Hong (2023) argues, proper use of ChatGPT will be a game changer for teaching approaches in higher education.

This study is among the few that provide empirical evidence combining student experiences and hypothesis testing, demonstrating that ChatGPT is user-friendly, facilitates academic writing in ICT for ELT courses, and fosters a positive attitude toward its use. These attributes not only enhance students' enjoyment of ChatGPT but also motivate them to integrate it into their academic activities. Furthermore, the study contributes to the limited experimental research on ChatGPT, particularly within the framework of the Technology Acceptance Model, highlighting its potential as an innovative tool for improving students' academic writing skills.

Conclusion

This study indicates students' acceptance of ChatGPT in writing courses. Students who find ChatGPT easy to operate tend to view it as more valuable and exhibit a more favorable attitude toward the shift from traditional learning methods to AI-assisted learning. This positive attitude toward change fosters a greater likelihood of students intending to act in accordance with these changes, specifically by consistently using ChatGPT for English language learning and recommending it to others. The ease of use of ChatGPT, facilitated by its user-friendly interface and ability to accommodate the Indonesian language, contributes significantly to its acceptance by EFL students in this study. ChatGPT provides aid throughout the writing process, from determining the topic and brainstorming to developing ideas, adding examples, analyzing and citing sources, correcting errors, and adjusting the length of the text.

In this study, every aspect of the Technology Acceptance Model is substantiated through students' real experiences. This ensured that the students' perceptions of the use of ChatGPT were genuinely rooted in their lived experiences rather than assumptions. Moreover, the findings were further validated by empirical results derived from statistical analysis, offering a more robust and reliable foundation. Future research should explore experimental designs that utilize ChatGPT in writing classes across other English language skills such as speaking, listening, and reading.

Disclosure statement

No potential conflict of interest was reported by the author(s).

ORCID

Urai Salam http://orcid.org/0000-0001-9508-4902

References

Alharbi, W. (2023). AI in the foreign language classroom: A pedagogical overview of automated writing assistance tools. *Education Research International*, *2023*, 1–15. https://doi.org/10.1155/2023/4253331

Almogren, A. S., Al-Rahmi, W. M., & Dahri, N. A. (2024). Exploring factors influencing the acceptance of ChatGPT in higher education: A smart education perspective. *Heliyon*, *10*(11), e31887. https://doi.org/10.1016/j.heliyon.2024.e31887

Askarbekuly, N., & Aničić, N. (2024). LLM examiner: Automating assessment in informal self-directed e-learning using ChatGPT. *Knowledge and Information Systems*, *66*(10), 6133–6150. https://doi.org/10.1007/s10115-024-02156-w

Baskara, R., & Mukarto, M. (2023). Exploring the implications of ChatGPT for language learning in higher education. *Indonesian Journal of English Language Teaching and Applied Linguistics*, *7*(2), 343–358. https://doi.org/10.21093/ijeltal.v7i2.1387

Creswell, J., & Clark, P. V. (2018). *Designing and conducting mixed methods research* (3rd ed.). SAGE Publications.

Dahri, N. A., Yahaya, N., Al-Rahmi, W. M., Aldraiweesh, A., Alturki, U., Almutairy, S., Shutaleva, A., & Soomro, R. B. (2024). Extended TAM based acceptance of AI-Powered ChatGPT for supporting metacognitive self-regulated learning in education: A mixed-methods study. *Heliyon*, *10*(8), e29317. https://doi.org/10.1016/j.heliyon.2024.e29317

Davis, F. D. (1989). Perceived usefulness, perceived ease of use, and user acceptance of information technology. *MIS Quarterly*, *13*(3), 319–340. https://doi.org/10.2307/249008

Du, J., & Alm, A. (2024). The impact of ChatGPT on English for Academic Purposes (EAP) students' language learning experience: A Self-Determination Theory perspective. *Education Sciences*, *14*(7), 726. https://doi.org/10.3390/educsci14070726

Duong, C. D., Vu, T. N., & Ngo, T. V. N. (2023). Applying a modified technology acceptance model to explain higher education students' usage of ChatGPT: A serial multiple mediation model with knowledge sharing as a moderator. *The International Journal of Management Education*, *21*(3), 100883. https://doi.org/10.1016/j.ijme.2023.100883

El Hefny, W., Mansy, Y., Abdallah, M., & Abdennadher, S. (2021). Jooka: A Bilingual chatbot for university admission In Á. Rocha, H. Adeli, G. Dzemyda, F. Moreira, A. M. Ramalho Correia, A.M. (Eds.), *Trends and applications in information systems and technologies* (pp. 671–681). Springer. https://doi.org/10.1007/978-3-030-72660-7_64

Fui-Hoon Nah, F., Zheng, R., Cai, J., Siau, K., & Chen, L. (2023). Generative AI and ChatGPT: Applications, challenges, and AI-human collaboration. *Journal of Information Technology Case and Application Research*, *25*(3), 277–304. https://doi.org/10.1080/15228053.2023.2233814

García-Alonso, E. M., León-Mejía, A. C., Sánchez-Cabrero, R., & Guzmán-Ordaz, R. (2024). Training and technology acceptance of ChatGPT in university students of social sciences: A netcoincidental analysis. *Behavioral Sciences*, *14*(7), 612. https://doi.org/10.3390/computers12080153

Guo, K., Wang, J., & Chu, S. K. W. (2022). Using chatbots to scaffold EFL students' argumentative writing. *Assessing Writing*, *54*, 100666. https://doi.org/10.1016/j.asw.2022.100666

Hasanein, A. M., & Sobaih, A. E. E. (2023). Drivers and consequences of ChatGPT use in higher education: Key stakeholder perspectives. *European Journal of Investigation in Health, Psychology and Education*, *13*(11), 2599–2614. https://doi.org/10.3390/ejihpe13110181

Hayashi, K., & Sato, T. (2024). *The effectiveness of ChatGPT in enhancing English language proficiency and reducing second language anxiety (L2)* [Paper presentation]. WorldCALL2023: Conference Proceedings (pp. 201–208). https://doi.org/10.22492/issn.2759-1182.2023.23

Hong, W. C. H. (2023). The impact of ChatGPT on foreign language teaching and learning: Opportunities in education and research. *Journal of Educational Technology and Innovation*, *5*(1), 36–45. https://doi.org/10.61414/jeti.v5i1.103

Jeon, J. (2023). Chatbot-assisted dynamic assessment (CA-DA) for L2 vocabulary learning and diagnosis. *Computer Assisted Language Learning*, *36*(7), 1338–1364. https://doi.org/10.1080/09588221.2021.1987272

Kasneci, E., Sessler, K., Küchemann, S., Bannert, M., Dementieva, D., Fischer, F., Gasser, U., Groh, G., Günnemann, S., Hüllermeier, E., Krusche, S., Kutyniok, G., Michaeli, T., Nerdel, C., Pfeffer, J., Poquet, O., Sailer, M., Schmidt, A., Seidel, T., … Kasneci, G. (2023). ChatGPT for good? On opportunities and challenges of large language models for education. *Learning and Individual Differences*, *103*, 102274. https://doi.org/10.1016/j.lindif.2023.102274

Kiger, M. E., & Varpio, L. (2020). Thematic analysis of qualitative data: AMEE Guide No. 131. *Medical Teacher*, *42*(8), 846–854. https://doi.org/10.1080/0142159X.2020.1755030

Kılıçkaya, F. (2020). Using a chatbot, replika, to practice writing through conversations in L2 English: A case study In M. Kruk & M. Peterson (Eds.), *New technological applications for foreign and second language learning and teaching* (pp. 221–238). IGI Global. https://doi.org/10.4018/978-1-7998-2591-3.ch011

Lai, C. Y., Cheung, K. Y., & Chan, C. S. (2023). Exploring the role of intrinsic motivation in ChatGPT adoption to support active learning: An extension of the technology acceptance model. *Computers and Education: Artificial Intelligence*, *5*, 100178. https://doi.org/10.1016/j.caeai.2023.100178

Liu, G., & Ma, C. (2024). Measuring EFL learners' use of ChatGPT in informal digital learning of English based on the technology acceptance model. *Innovation in Language Learning and Teaching*, *18*(2), 125–138. https://doi.org/10.1080/17501229.2023.2240316

Nagata, R., Hashiguchi, T., & Sadoun, D. (2020). *Is the simplest chatbot effective in English writing learning assistance?* [Paper presentation]. Computational Linguistics: 16th International Conference of the Pacific Association for Computational Linguistics, PACLING 2019, *Hanoi, Vietnam*, October 11–13, 2019. Revised Selected Papers 16 (pp. 245–256). Springer Singapore. https://doi.org/10.1007/978-981-15-6168-9_21

Niloy, A. C., Akter, S., Sultana, N., Sultana, J., & Rahman, S. I. U. (2024). Is ChatGPT a menace for creative writing ability? An experiment. *Journal of Computer Assisted Learning*, *40*(2), 919–930. https://doi.org/10.1111/jcal.12929

Nugroho, A., Andriyanti, E., Widodo, P., & Mutiaraningrum, I. (2024). Students' appraisals post-ChatGPT use: Students' narrative after using ChatGPT for writing. *Innovations in Education and Teaching International*, 1–13. https://doi.org/10.1080/14703297.2024.2319184

Phuong, H. P. X. (2024). Using ChatGPT in English language learning: A Study on IT students' attitudes, habits, and perceptions. *Online Submission*, *4*, 55–68. (1), https://doi.org/10.54855/ijte.24414

Punar Özçelik, N., & Yangın Ekşi, G. (2024). Cultivating writing skills: The role of ChatGPT as a learning assistant—A case study. *Smart Learning Environments*, *11*(1), 10. https://doi.org/10.1186/s40561-024-00296-8

Qasem, F., Ghaleb, M., Mahdi, H. S., Al Khateeb, A., & Al Fadda, H. (2023). Dialog chatbot as an interactive online tool in enhancing ESP vocabulary learning. *Saudi Journal of Language Studies*, *3*(2), 76–86. https://doi.org/10.1108/SJLS-10-2022-0072

Saif, N., Khan, S. U., Shaheen, I., ALotaibi, F. A., Alnfiai, M. M., & Arif, M. (2024). Chat-GPT; validating Technology Acceptance Model (TAM) in education sector via ubiquitous learning mechanism. *Computers in Human Behavior*, *154*, 108097. https://doi.org/10.1016/j.chb.2023.108097

Salloum, S. A., Aljanada, R. A., Alfaisal, A. M., A., Saidat, M. R., & Alfaisal, R. (2024). Exploring the acceptance of ChatGPT for translation: An extended TAM model approach In A. Al-Marzouqi, S. A. Salloum, M. Al-Saidat, A. Aburayya, & B. Gupta (Eds.), *Artificial intelligence in education: The power and dangers of ChatGPT in the classroom* (pp. 527–542). Springer Science and Business Media Deutschland GmbH. https://doi.org/10.1007/978-3-031-52280-2_33.

Shaengchart, Y. (2023). A conceptual review of TAM and ChatGPT usage intentions among higher education students. *Advance Knowledge for Executives*, *2*(3), 1–7. https://ssrn.com/abstract=4581231

Shaikh, S., Yayilgan, S. Y., Klimova, B., & Pikhart, M. (2023). Assessing the usability of ChatGPT for formal English language learning. *European Journal of Investigation in Health, Psychology and Education*, *13*(9), 1937–1960. https://doi.org/10.3390/ejihpe13090140

Songsiengchai, S., Sereerat, B. O., & Watananimitgul, W. (2023). Leveraging Artificial Intelligence (AI): Chat GPT for effective English language learning among Thai students. *English Language Teaching*, *16*(11), 68. https://doi.org/10.5539/elt.v16n11p68

Sulissusiawan, A., & Salam, U. (2017). Students' use of online resources to enhance learning endeavors. *International Journal of Virtual and Personal Learning Environments*, *7*(2), 44–53. https://doi.org/10.4018/IJVPLE.2017070104

Tsai, C. Y., Lin, Y. T., & Brown, I. K. (2024). Impacts of ChatGPT-assisted writing for EFL English majors: Feasibility and challenges. *Education and Information Technologies*, 1–19. http://dx.doi.org/10.1007/s10639-024-12722-y

Wang, X., & Feng, Y. (2023, September). *An experimental study of ChatGPT-assisted improvement of Chinese college students' English reading skills: A case study of Dear Life* [Paper presentation]. Proceedings of the 15th International Conference on Education Technology and Computers (pp. 21–26). https://doi.org/10.1145/3629296.3629300

Xiao, Y., & Zhi, Y. (2023). An exploratory study of EFL learners' use of ChatGPT for language learning tasks: Experience and perceptions. *Languages*, *8*(3), 212. https://doi.org/10.3390/languages8030212

Xiao, Q. (2024, April). *ChatGPT as an Artificial Intelligence (AI) writing assistant for EFL learners: An exploratory study of its effects on English writing proficiency* [Paper presentation]. Proceedings of the 2024 9th International Conference on Information and Education Innovations (pp. 51–56). https://doi.org/10.1145/3664934.3664946

Yang, H., Kim, H., Lee, J. H., & Shin, D. (2022). Implementation of an AI chatbot as an English conversation partner in EFL speaking classes. *ReCALL*, *34*(3), 327–343. https://doi.org/10.1017/S0958344022000039

Yang, L., & Li, R. (2024). ChatGPT for L2 learning: Currentstatus and implications. *System*, *124*, 103351. https://doi.org/10.1016/j.system.2024.103351

Zhu, C., Sun, M., Luo, J., Li, T., & Wang, M. (2023). How to harness the potential of ChatGPT in Education? *Knowledge Management & E-Learning: An International Journal*, *15*(2), 133–152. https://doi.org/10.34105/j.kmel.2023.15.008

Appendix A: TAM questionnaire

No	Questionnaire	Strongly disagree	Disagree	Neutral	Agree	Strongly agree
	Perceived Ease of Use					
1	ChatGPT is clear and understandable.					
2	I find it easy to use ChatGPT to do what I want it to do					
3	I find ChatGPT easy to use					
	Perceived Usefulness					
4	Using ChatGPT improves my learning of English Writing					
5	Using ChatGPT increase my productivity in English writing practice					
6	ChatGPT is excellent tool to improve the quality of my English writing.					
	Attitude Toward Change					
7	ChatGPT is interesting					
8	I hope my learning activity is related to the use of ChatGPT					
	Behavioral Intention					
9	I will use ChatGPT in the future.					
10	I plan to use ChatGPT often					

Open-ended questionnaire

1. 1 According to your experience, in what ways did ChatGPT assist you in writing?
2. What convenience do you gain from using ChatGPT in learning writing?
3. Would you recommend the use of ChatGPT to friends and others? Why?

Assessing AI and Human Writing Skills: A Comparative Analysis of Pre-Service Teachers' Perceptions

Maria Navío-Inglés, Sergio Tirado-Olivares, Javier del Olmo-Muñoz and Jesús Guzmán Mora

ABSTRACT

Artificial intelligence (AI), specifically conversational AI, is increasingly utilized to enhance writing skills, necessitating future teachers' awareness of its capabilities for implementation. The present mixed-methods study explores the ability of AI to write a summary and an argumentative text and pre-service teachers' perceptions of it. A total of 154 pre-service teachers evaluated two texts generated by ChatGPT and two written by another student previously anonymized. The results show that they rated the AI-generated texts significantly higher overall and regarding linguistic parameters like text structure. Additionally, they generally consider that the human-written text conveys more emotions, while the AI text would deserve a better grade in an exam. However, many participants struggled to correctly identify the author of each text, which highlights the need to prepare them for the possibilities of current AI to take advantage of it.

Introduction

One of the main objectives across the different educational stages is the development and improvement of writing skills. Nonetheless, it is a challenge that is not being tackled successfully, as it is not given the attention its complexity requires, nor is it approached in an effective manner (Simón Parra, 2015). In an attempt to face this situation, the possibilities of emerging technologies in the educational field are being explored. Among them, the potential of artificial intelligence (hereinafter AI) in the form of chatbots or conversational AI to support the improvement of expression and language use has been investigated in recent years (Okonkwo & Ade-Ibijola, 2021).

The advances related to AI are having a considerable impact not only on today's society, but also on the educational landscape, as highlighted by the relevance given to it in different international reports (e.g., Pelletier et al., 2024), which give generative AI a prominent role also in the future of education. This makes it necessary to explore the possibilities offered by generative AI, which is characterized by producing new content in a similar way to that which a human being would generate through a series of instructions (Lim et al., 2023). Generative AI models such as OpenAI's ChatGPT exemplify this capability and offer a transformative potential in educational environments, as evidenced by the revolution unleashed after the release of its 3.5 version at the end of 2022. However, the exploration of their educational potential requires mastery and knowledge of its capabilities and risks on the part of teachers (Lo, 2023, World Economic Forum, 2024).

Based on the above, the present study analyzes the ability of the generative AI tool ChatGPT-3.5 to write summaries and argumentative texts in comparison to the ability of a person to perform the same task. In addition, the perceptions of pre-service teachers about such a contrast are examined. For this purpose, a group of pre-service teachers was asked to evaluate texts produced by both the AI system and another peer according to a set of linguistic criteria contained in two rubrics. To do this, the texts were previously anonymized. Subsequently, participants' beliefs on the matter were collected through three open-ended questions.

Conversational AI in education

Since the early conceptualizations of AI in the mid-twentieth century, the development of new tools has given rise to an interest in AI's introduction in many fields (Kasneci et al., 2023; Zhang & Aslan, 2021). Among the various AI-powered tools available, conversational AI systems, and particularly chatbots, stand out for their ability to engage in meaningful conversations with the user (Shawar & Atwell, 2007) and therefore try to replicate an interaction just as it would occur between two people. This process is possible thanks to Natural Language Processing (NLP), which enables these systems to comprehend language through speech or writing (Bansal & Khan, 2018). NLP alludes to "using computational techniques to learn, understand, and produce human language content" (Hirschberg & Manning, 2015, p. 261). The goal of this process, as the authors note, can be either to improve communication between people, like with translators, or to enable communication between humans and machines, as is the case with chatbots.

In order to achieve those aims, different language models have been developed. As explained in Chang et al. (2024), these are computational models capable of understanding and generating text in a particular language, trained to predict word sequences and produce text when given an input. Those trained on huge amounts of data are known as large language models (LLMs) (Kasneci et al., 2023), among which we find generative pretrained transformers (GPT), a model that generates new data from the information provided in its training. Specifically, it undergoes an unsupervised training phase with unlabeled information and a supervised training phase for more specific tasks (Budzianowski & Vulić, 2019; Radford et al., 2018). This is the case for some of the most well-known conversational AI systems to date, such as Open AI's ChatGPT.

The implementation of this and other kinds of AI can potentially affect education in a variety of positive and negative ways. However, the debate about the opportunities and hazards of AI in the educational field is not new, as in the decade of 1980 authors like Ennals (1982) and Yazdani and Lawler (1986) already defended the usefulness of AI. Since then, many studies regarding its utilization and the consequences of the introduction of this technology in this domain have been undertaken. As revealed by the systematic review conducted by Okonkwo and Ade-Ibijọla (2021) focusing on chatbots, they have been used for administrative tasks, assessment, research and development, and advice. However, as the authors state, they are mainly utilized for teaching and learning support. In this regard, some investigations show that chatbots can be used for tasks such as providing course content (Cunningham-Nelson et al., 2019), for collaborative activities (Tegos et al., 2014) or even for giving feedback to their users (Kulik & Fletcher, 2016).

Recent studies (e.g., Kasneci et al., 2023; Lo, 2023; Zhang & Tur, 2023) have explored the integration of ChatGPT in educational contexts, highlighting its potential and challenges. Despite these existing studies, further research is still needed to address specific aspects of the constantly evolving generative AI (Cong-Lem et al., 2024). This evolution implies changes and new possibilities of usage, which should be explored to guarantee a successful introduction of this kind of system in education. In addition, research indicates that teacher understanding and preparation are crucial to the successful integration of AI tools in the classroom. Studies have shown that, although teachers generally have a positive attitude toward AI in education (Polak et al., 2022), there is a need for continuous professional development to improve their digital and AI-related skills (Kasneci et al., 2023; Zhang & Tur, 2023). Consequently, assessing their knowledge about chatbots and AI systems becomes essential to ensure that these technologies are used effectively in education.

Chatbots and writing skills

Developing writing competence is a process that entails some difficulty for students (Graham, 2018). The correct acquisition of this skill is perceived as a challenge that still requires an effective response (Cassany, 1999), as evidenced by the low quality of students' texts observed in Primary Education, which even extends to higher educational levels (Fernández Merino, 2015). Its proper development involves a long and complex path, as it comprises multiple operations and factors and the combination of linguistic knowledge with the mastery of the processes linked to the production of texts (Godwin-Jones, 2022; Simón Parra, 2015).

This has led to a search for resources and strategies to address this complexity, such as using emerging technologies (Williams & Beam, 2019). In the case of conversational AI, its use for educational purposes is not new and, for language teaching in particular, the effects of its inclusion in the development of aspects such as oral expression, vocabulary acquisition, grammar and even writing have been explored (e.g., Hwang & Chang, 2023; Kim et al., 2020). Song and Song (2023) mention the potential of this type of tool to support the improvement of writing skills and highlight the possibilities of ChatGPT for this purpose. Similarly, authors such as Barrot (2024) and Huang and Tan (2023) allude to the effectiveness of the same chatbot in enhancing the development of this skill, contributing, for example, to achieve more coherent and cohesive texts.

In this regard, it is worth highlighting again the recent advances in the field of generative AI. Compared to previous chatbots and language models, tools such as ChatGPT are characterized by a greater capacity to process language and generate new information by working on the data they have available (Pavlik, 2023). This implies the production of texts with an increasingly human-like expression (Dale, 2021; Lund & Wang, 2023), which has led to the emergence of studies focused on analyzing the ability of conversational AI to write human-like texts and discriminating AI-written texts from texts written by humans (Gao et al., 2023; Guo et al., 2023). In this way, researchers have attempted to determine some distinguishing features that allow the differentiation of AI from a human writer. These features are often linked to issues such as the expression of emotions or the use of personal pronouns (Guo et al., 2023; Mitrović et al., 2023).

However, further research about the functionality and educational possibilities of chatbots is still needed (Okonkwo & Ade-Ibijola, 2021). In order to harness the potential of current tools such as ChatGPT for improving students' writing skills, it is essential that teachers are aware of their potential and their dangers, as they are the ones who will implement them in the classroom. Consequently, their knowledge of this type of AI tool and its expressive skills should be analyzed. In this context, this study has two objectives: to examine and compare the writing skills of generative AI and pre-service teachers, and to investigate the latter's viewpoints on these matters. Thus, the research questions of the present study are as follows:

RQ.1. Do the writing skills of a generative AI differ from those of a pre-service teacher in producing a summary and an argumentative text?

RQ.2. What are pre-service teachers' perceptions of AI-generated texts and human-written texts, and what attributes do they associate with each writing style?

Materials and methods

Design

To address the research objectives established, a mixed methods study was conducted. This design intended to compare AI proficiency in text writing with that of pre-service teachers trained in language teaching. In addition, it attempted to assess these pre-service teachers' conception of AI-generated texts.

Participants

This study was conducted at a Spanish university. In particular, a total of 155 pre-service teachers (115 females and 40 males) from the Faculty of Education of the University of Castilla-La Mancha participated in the study. The predominance of the female gender among the participants is justified by the fact that, traditionally, the number of women studying in the education branch tends to be higher than that of men (Navarro-Guzmán & Casero-Martínez, 2012). All the participants were being instructed in the teaching of the first language for compulsory education students. After studying the first language, and therefore developing their writing skills since the early stages of education, pre-service teachers in this university have two subjects focused on how the language is structured and how to teach it to their pupils. However, it should be noted that, as previously stated, authors such as Simón Parra (2015) note that insufficient attention is paid to writing instruction and students carry over deficiencies in this regard even in higher education.

Prior to the intervention, participants were informed that they were going to be part of an investigation and were required to read and sign an informed consent form. To this end, they previously had the opportunity to ask any relevant questions. In addition, they were told that they could revoke their consent at any time. Data from those students who did not sign the informed consent were not used in the study. This procedure aimed to comply with the ethical standards established by the American Psychological Association (APA) throughout the study.

Procedure

Phase 1. Writing of texts by pre-service teachers

Two brief writing activities were selected for completion by pre-service teachers. To ensure that the activities were adapted to the sample under study, they were taken from the official university entrance exam of the autonomous community where the study was conducted. Specifically, they belonged to the exam that assessed students' knowledge of Language and Literature. In addition, selecting activities from a university entrance exam ensured that the contents were already known to university students and that they had been prepared by professors who were experts in the field of study. Both activities were based on the reading of a text. The first one asked to summarize its content and the second one involved writing an argumentative text in which students had to express their opinion about an idea drawn from the initial reading. These tasks were chosen deliberately so one of them was more mechanical and required more objective writing, while the other one was mainly based on subjectivity and expressing one's own point of view. Participants had 50 minutes to complete these activities. To ensure that they did not use any type of support, these tasks were carried out in a controlled space within the students' own faculty under exam-like conditions.

After that, the researchers in this study evaluated the texts produced by the participants and selected the highest-quality set of activities (see Appendix 1) to guarantee an equitable comparison against AI's abilities. The chosen texts would be used later for students to evaluate human and AI writing. The author of the chosen activities was removed from the next phases of the study to preserve the proper conditions for its development.

Phase 2. Text generation by ChatGPT

ChatGPT was asked to carry out the same activities as the participants in the study (see Appendix 1). For this purpose, it was provided with the same statements and indications previously given to the students. Therefore, this means that ChatGPT had access to the text they had to read to complete both activities, as well as the instructions for each task. Both the texts generated by ChatGPT and those from pre-service teachers were transferred to a word processor without modifying the content and were formatted in the same way to prevent revealing authorship.

Phase 3. Comparison of AI-generated text vs. human text

First, both activities completed by ChatGPT and by the student were presented to the rest of the participants along with the activity statement so that they understood where they came from. From there, they were asked to evaluate both summaries and argumentative texts. To standardize this task, they were provided with the rubric explained in section "Instruments". It should be noted that the pre-service teachers, at the time of this evaluation, had not been informed that one of the two texts had been generated by an AI tool.

Phase 4. Collection of students' conceptions

Subsequently, once all participants had evaluated the activities using the rubric, they were asked three questions that enabled the collection of qualitative data. It is from these questions that we could learn about the teachers' viewpoint on the potential of generative AI. The first questions asked the participants to assess and justify the academic performance and emotionality of the texts without revealing the author of each one, and then, the last one asked them to choose which text could be written by the AI and explain the features that led to their decision.

It should be noted that it was only in the last question, and not before, that the students were told they were in front of an AI-generated text. A summary of the procedure can be seen in Figure 1.

Instruments

The assessment of the texts was done through the adaptation of two rubrics. The first one, applied to the summary, was based on the instrument validated by Argüelles Álvarez (2004). It consisted of the first four items of the original scale on a four-point Likert-type scale (1 = poor, 4 = very well), focusing on analyzing content, organization in terms of coherence and structure of expository texts, vocabulary accuracy, and the use of paraphrasing and linguistic correctness.

For the second activity, concerning the argumentative text, the first four items retrieved from the instrument validated by Martínez-Huamán et al. (2022) were used. These items evaluated the understandability and how it was reflected in the text, structure in accordance with the standards of an argumentative text, content and personal contribution quality, and grammar and vocabulary. As in the first activity, this was a four-point Likert-type scale (1 = deficient, 4 = very good).

As these were reductions of the original questionnaires and some items were removed because they did not fit the needs and purposes of this research, their reliability was confirmed by Cronbach's alpha statistic for

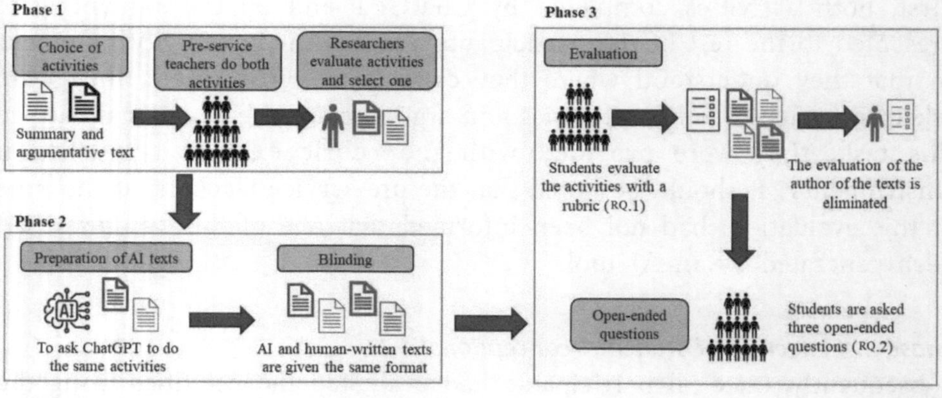

Figure 1. Summary of the procedure followed.

both the first ($\alpha = .756$) and the second questionnaire ($\alpha = .747$). Finally, the open-ended questions were based on those developed by Tirado-Olivares et al. (2023), which were designed for a similar sample and research objectives:

- Which texts do you think deserve a higher score on an exam? Why?
- Which ones are capable of conveying more emotions and feelings?
- Which of the set of two exercises would you say was written by a person and which one would you say was written by artificial intelligence? What led you to decide to whom each set of answers belongs to?

Data analysis

Subsequently, data gathered were coded and analyzed using two distinct software tools. Firstly, SPSS version 28 was employed for quantitative data. This software facilitated both descriptive and inferential analyses. Since the data were ordinal, a Wilcoxon signed-rank test was conducted to address the first research objective. To analyze the effect size, Rosenthal's *r* was used. For its interpretation, Field's (2009) criteria was used, wherein 0.1 is considered small, 0.3 a medium and 0.5 a large effect size, respectively.

For qualitative data, specifically the responses to open-ended questions, Atlas.ti version 24 was used, a software designed for qualitative research that also includes AI. An inductive analysis was performed as there were no pre-established categories for the codes. This approach aimed to address the second research objective, focusing on the viewpoint of the pre-service teachers who participated in the study. For this, two researchers from the team performed the content analysis of the data based on the intentional coding proposed by the AI. Any uncertainties or disagreements were resolved through discussion. In the results section, the codes are italicized for easier identification.

Lastly, responses to the open-ended questions were compared, and a statistical inferential analysis was conducted using the chi-squared test in SPSS. Responses were coded as follows: for the first question, if students believed that the human-written text deserved a higher score, it was coded as (1). If they thought the AI text deserved a higher score, it was coded as (2). If they believed both texts deserved the same score, it was coded as (0). The same coding scheme was applied to determine which text conveyed more emotions and feelings. For the third question, responses were coded as (1) whether participants guessed correctly which text was generated by an AI, and (2) whether they did not guess correctly. For all analyses, a confidence interval of 95% was used.

Results

The results are structured into sections, each corresponding to a specific research objective. The first analysis was conducted to compare the scores assigned to each set of texts by the participants (RQ.1). This analysis provides insights into pre-service teachers' criteria for evaluating the quality of the texts based on the supplied rubric. The second analysis focused on understanding the students' perceptions about the two texts presented (RQ.2). It aimed to determine why students might have rated one set of texts higher than the other, which set they believed conveyed more emotions, and their views on the ability of a conversational AI tool to produce both a similar summary and an argumentative text.

Comparison of writing skills between a pre-service teacher and the generative AI ChatGPT (RQ.1)

In relation to the first research objective, scores given by pre-service teachers to each set of texts and the items evaluated are presented in Tables 1 and 2. In addition, to evaluate if the differences obtained were statistically significant, an inferential analysis using the Wilcoxon signed-rank test was carried out. Starting with the first activity (related to the ability to prepare a summary text), the data obtained are shown in Table 1.

The results obtained show that participants, when assessing linguistic aspects such as organization, content and lexical range, scored the text generated by ChatGPT higher than that of their classmate. In this regard, it should be recalled that they did not know that one of the texts had been written by a generative AI. These differences obtained can be observed both in the overall score and on each aspect evaluated. Importantly, these differences were statistically significant in the average score (with a small to medium effect size) and in two of the items assessed (content and organization), again, with a small to medium effect size in both cases. With regard to the results obtained in relation to the argumentative text, certain similarities to the previous case emerge (Table 2).

Although the participants rated the student's argumentative text better than the student's summary, they again scored the AI-generated

Table 1. Scores given by participants to both summary texts.

		Summary text						
		Student text		AI text				
Item	*N*	*M*	*SD*	*M*	*SD*	*Z*	*p*	*r*
Content	154	2.96	.69	3.14	.74	−2.24	0.0248	0,18
Organization	154	2.87	.69	3.08	.74	−2.62	0.0087	0,21
Vocabulary	154	2.81	.92	2.98	.73	−1.81	0.0705	0,15
Use of language	154	2.81	.91	2.94	.78	− 1.33	0.1851	0,11
Mean score	154	2.86	.62	3.03	.55	−2.71	0.0067	0,22

Table 2. Scores given by participants to both argumentative texts.

		Argumentative text						
		Student text		AI text				
Item	*N*	*M*	*SD*	*M*	*SD*	*Z*	*P*	*r*
Comprehension	154	3.06	.72	3.42	.65	−4.57	<.0001	0.37
Structure	154	2.68	.79	3.09	.79	−4.17	<.0001	0.34
Content-personal proposal	154	3.16	.71	3.22	.69	−0.79	0.4277	0.06
Grammatical correctness	154	3.18	.72	3.25	.73	−0.83	0.4066	0.07
Mean score	154	3.02	.55	3.25	.52	−3.55	<.0001	0.29

argumentative text higher. Indeed, upon reviewing the data derived from the inferential analysis, it is observed that the significant differences in the overall mean score are more pronounced than those associated with the summary text. In fact, a medium effect was found in this case. Furthermore, two statistically significant differences emerge once again in favor of the AI-generated text in two of the evaluated aspects: comprehension and structure, with a medium effect size too. This reaffirms the findings, underscoring the effectiveness of the AI model in generating high-quality text.

Analysis of pre-service teachers' perception of generative AI discursive skills vs. those of an individual (RQ.2)

Following the evaluation of both the AI-generated activities and those developed by a fellow pre-service teacher, the open-ended questions facilitated a deeper exploration of the pre-service teachers' perspectives, thereby shedding light on the scores previously assigned according to the rubric. The first question was, "Which activities do you think deserve a higher score on an exam? Why?". Based on the coding previously noted, only 3.3% of the participants assigned equal scores to both activities. In contrast, 66.2% of the participants believed that the activities done by ChatGPT warranted a higher rating. Meanwhile, activities developed by a peer received a higher score from 29.6% of the participants. This data suggests a strong preference for the activities produced by a generative AI, underscoring the potential of AI not only to write a suitable summary but also an argumentative text based on the given instructions.

Upon examination of the justifications provided in the open-ended questions with the Atlas.ti software, the students considered the AI-generated activities to deserve a better score due to, among other aspects, their *enhanced structuring*: "I consider that answer 2 [AI] should be better valued, given that it presents a better expression of ideas, uses more appropriate language and presents greater coherence in the discourse" (S.13). Furthermore, students discerned that the second set of texts exhibited *superior clarity in the exposition* and *comprehension of the original text*: "Answer 2 deserved better marks than answer 1 because it presents the ideas in a clearer and more orderly manner, discriminating the most irrelevant information. In addition, it includes an opinion supported by the information provided in the text." (S.48). The students also appreciated the *better language usage* by the AI: "The second one, since I consider that it has added more relevant information than the first one, and the vocabulary and connectors are better employed, as in the personal opinion: better written and with more arguments." (S.61). In this context, its *lexical richness* was particularly noteworthy: "It would deserve more marks under my point of view the answer no. 2, due to the fact that the content is more adequate, and its vocabulary is more cultured." (S.119).

Regarding the second question "Which ones are capable of transmitting more emotions and feelings?", the responses revealed that 55.3% of the participants believed that human-generated texts had a greater ability to convey emotions, while 28.9% chose AI-generated texts and 15.8% believed that both did it equally. These data suggest that the majority of participants perceived that a human-generated text is more effective in eliciting emotions compared to an AI-generated text. To further investigate this, a chi-square test of independence was conducted to examine the relationship between top-rated activities (question 1) and the ability to convey emotion (question 2). The results of this test revealed no significant relationship between the two variables ($X^2(4) = 5.32$; $p = 0.2558$). To calculate the effect size, the Cramér's V (V) was used. In this case, a V of .133 was obtained, thus a small effect size can be considered. Thus, the higher score given to the AI activities was not clearly related to a greater ability to convey emotions from the participants' point of view (Table 3).

However, it should be noted that the percentage of participants who scored both sets of texts equally or even rated the AI-generated texts higher in this second question is not negligible. These findings seem to suggest that, regardless of the choice in question 1, student activities are perceived as more powerful in conveying emotions. When evaluating this capacity

Table 3. Crosstabs table of higher score and ability to convey emotions.

			Convey emotions			
			Both equally	Student texts	AI texts	Total
Higher score	Both equally	Count	2	3	0	5
		% within question 2	8.3%	3.6%	0%	3.3%
	Student texts	Count	5	24	17	46
		% within question 2	20.8%	28.9%	38.6%	30.5%
	AI texts	Count	17	56	27	100
		% within question 2	70.8%	67.5%	61.4%	66.2%
Total		Count	24	83	44	
		% within question 2	100%	100%	100%	

to evoke emotions, pre-service teachers rely on subjective variables such as the expression of *personal opinions*: "Answer number 2 [AI] shows more feelings because the first one is only a summary of the text. In the second one it is the reader's opinion." (S.57) or "The first subject starts giving his opinion from the first two lines" (S.62), thereby highlighting the diversity of perspectives on this matter, as evidenced by the reported frequencies. Moreover, some participants also determined *formality* affected the capacity to convey emotions: "The first answer. Because he speaks more informally, following his own pattern of opinion and his own words." (S.70).

Finally, focusing on the last of the questions "Which set of two exercises would you say was written by a person and which one would you say was written by artificial intelligence? What led you to decide to whom each answer belongs to?", the students' responses indicate high ability to identify AI-generated text. Specifically, 76.2% of the participants correctly identified AI-generated activities, while 23.8% incorrectly attributed these to their peer. A chi-square test of independence was conducted to determine whether there was a relationship between the higher rating of the text in question 1 and students' identification of activities that could have been generated by an AI tool (question 3). At this time, a significant association was found between both answers (X^2 (2) = 22.34; p <.001. Additionally, a medium effect size was found (V = .386). Then, those participants who indicate that the AI texts are the best ones, also attribute authorship more correctly (75.4% of the participants). On the other hand, those who do not identify correctly assign a higher value to the human text (see Table 4).

Similarly, a significant relation was also found between which activities could have been done by an AI (question 3) and their capabilities to convey emotions (question 2) (X^2 (2) = 7.15; p=.028) with a small effect size (V=. 219). As can be seen in Table 5, there seems to be an association between correctly identifying the text written by ChatGPT and assigning a greater capacity to arouse emotions to the activities developed by the classmate, as 59.3% of the participants that correctly identified the author of each set of texts think the pre-service teacher's ones convey more emotions, and only 23.9% opted for AI's texts. However, among those who

Table 4. Crosstabs table of higher score and identification AI texts.

			Identification AI texts		
			Not correct	Correct	Total
Higher score	Both equally	Count	0	5	5
		% within question 3	0.0%	4.4%	3.3%
	Student text	Count	22	23	45
		% within question 3	61,1%	20.2%	30.0%
	AI text	Count	14	86	100
		% within question 3	38.9%	75.4%	66.7%
Total		Count	36	114	150
		% within question 3	100%	100%	100%

Table 5. Crosstabs table of convey emotions capacity and identification AI texts.

			Identification AI texts		
			Not correct	Correct	Total
Convey emotions	Both equally	Count	4	19	23
		% within question 3	11.1%	16.8%	15.4%
	Student text	Count	15	67	82
		% within question 3	41,7%	59.3%	55.0%
	AI text	Count	17	27	44
		% within question 3	47.2%	23.9%	29.5%
Total		Count	36	113	149
		% within question 3	100%	100%	100%

do not correctly identify the text, opinions are mixed, as 41.7% of those who chose the incorrect set of texts believe that the students' texts convey more emotions, while 47.2% think the same of those written by AI.

In the analysis of the justifications provided for this final question, it is noteworthy that participants attribute the authorship of the first activities to a human, citing a perceived increase in *emotional expression* as opposed to a *better language usage* attributed to an AI: "The first response appears to be authored by a human due to its less formal vocabulary, clear stance, and expressive emotional content. The subsequent response seems to be the product of an AI, given its more formal vocabulary, well-structured composition, and appropriate use of punctuation." (S.14). Furthermore, participants frequently highlighted the *impersonal tone*, *lexical richness*, and *comprehensive content* of the AI-generated texts. This observation is evident in different answers, such as the following one: "I surmise that the second response is AI-generated due to its mechanical and perfectionist nature. Conversely, the alternative responses exhibit a more emotional perspective, which is beyond the capabilities of an AI." (S.144) or "The first response seems to be human authored as it frequently uses the phrase 'this text (verb) us' [referring to the use of 1st plural person in text typing in the mother tongue], leading me to believe it was written by a person. It also presents a more personal opinion. In contrast, the second response appears to be AI-generated as it distills the most pertinent information using sophisticated vocabulary." (S.153).

It should be noted that the same justifications can be seen when the participants incorrectly identify the author of each set of texts: "Response one has been written by an artificial intelligence, as the answers are well written, but it writes them in an objective way. Whereas answer two has been written by a person, as it has some mistakes and the second question is more emotional, and human beings are like that." (S.89) or "I think response 1 was written by artificial intelligence. This is because the language is too specialized, and the comprehension of the text is too perfect for it to have been written by a student." (S.53). All this underscores the perceptions of participants regarding the authorship of text, revealing a dichotomy between emotional expressiveness attributed to humans and formal, comprehensive writing attributed to AI.

Discussion and conclusions

The use of chatbots to optimize the language teaching-learning process has been documented in the literature over the last few years (Hwang & Chang, 2023; Kim et al., 2020). However, recent progress in generative conversational AI tools requires being informed about their potential and risks. These tools can generate increasingly human-like text (Dale, 2021; Lund & Wang, 2023), using language similarly to how a human being would. In line with this, the results obtained in the present research show that pre-service teachers consider that ChatGPT can write both a summary and an argumentative text even better than another pre-service teacher based on linguistic criteria. These results are in line with the findings in the current literature. Examples of this are studies such as those conducted by Guo et al. (2023) and Mitrović et al. (2023), which also highlight some traits that could help discern between AI and a person, many of which are somehow related to expressing subjectivity (e.g. personal opinion, use of personal pronouns). Nonetheless, similar to the findings reported by Tirado-Olivares et al. (2023), ChatGPT has been able to write a text prototypically based on expressing an opinion with better results than a pre-service teacher. One explanation for this could be found in the low profiency in writing that authors such as Simón Parra (2015) claim is already perceived in Primary Education and extends to higher educational levels. Consequently, AI could probably have a natural advantage in terms of writing quality due to its training process and access to information.

When focusing on the different items of the rubrics, significant differences in favor of AI stand out regarding the structuring of information in each text. This would contrast with the belief that AI is useful as a support for addressing mainly superficial aspects of writing, such as spelling (Stevenson, 2016; Wilson & Czik, 2016), as it appears that the novel generative AI can be more efficient than a human when it comes to addressing a deep aspect such as the organization and coherence of the writing. In this regard, Herbold et al. (2023) note, in the specific case of argumentative texts, that essays written by ChatGPT follow the structure usually sought, which is in line with the results of the present study.

Regarding the second objective, pre-service teachers tend to perceive the AI-generated set of texts as better responses to an exam. The justifications provided by the participants for their positive assessment of AI cover different writing and language aspects including structure, lexical richness, language use, clarity and better comprehension of the original text. Thus, it encompasses both shallow and deeper aspects of writing.

The results obtained seem to align with what is reported in relation to other language skills. de Winter (2024) tested the reading comprehension of the GPT-3.5 model and its score was comparable to the average score of students at the same level of education as those in the present study.

At the same time, more than half of the pre-service teachers that participated in this investigation believe the human-written text is capable of conveying more emotions. In this sense, authors like Mitrović et al. (2023) explain that conversational AI systems like ChatGPT are less emotional than humans in their writing. Nevertheless, it is noteworthy that a significant proportion of students, precisely 28.9%, identified the tasks performed by ChatGPT as the ones that are best at conveying emotions, what can indicate that this feature might not be completely defining when telling apart human-written texts from AI-written texts. This could again be interpreted as an indication of the evolving sophistication of AI language usage, which appears to be converging toward human-like patterns (Lund & Wang, 2023).

When students are asked to identify which text belongs to each author, most of them do it correctly. Nevertheless, almost a quarter of the pre-service teachers get it wrong, which underpins the need for more studies that broaden the frame for the correct introduction of chatbots in education (Okonkwo & Ade-Ibijola, 2021), since learners and teachers might not be fully aware of the capabilities of these tools. Students' explanations seem to tend to associate emotional expressions and grammatical forms that show subjectivity, such as personal pronouns like "us", with human authorship, while attributing objectivity to AI. Again, this is in line with the distinguishing features some authors refer to (Guo et al. 2023; Mitrović et al., 2023). Moreover, they associate better composition with the set of texts developed by ChatGPT, which corresponds with the results obtained in the rubric before they even knew that one set of activities had not been performed by a person. Therefore, pre-service teachers indirectly assume that AI writes better than they do.

Considering all the above, according to participants' evaluations based on linguistic criteria, conversational AI systems such as ChatGPT appear to be capable of writing different kinds of texts that surpass those developed by pre-service teachers. AI's efficiency in structuring and organizing challenges the perception that it especially addresses superficial aspects of writing (Stevenson, 2016; Wilson & Czik, 2016). Besides that, even though a big proportion of the participants were able to correctly identify an AI-generated text when informed that one of the tasks they were evaluating was produced by an AI, the distinction between AI and human writing is not so clear for some students. Consequently, not all future teachers are fully cognizant of the current capabilities of AI systems regarding writing skills.

This should have important implications for teacher training, as educators must be equipped not only with the skills necessary to integrate AI tools into their teaching practices, but also with a thorough understanding of them to critically evaluate AI-generated content, recognizing its limitations and potential biases to avoid misinformation or reinforce existing biases. As AI can aid in the teaching-learning process of writing competence by means of instant feedback and guidance (Godwin Jones, 2022), proper preparation will also enable teachers to leverage AI to improve students' organizational and coherence skills in writing.

Limitations and future research

The present investigation raises new questions that deserve to be further explored in future research. Firstly, it would be valuable to include other widely available AI systems, such as Copilot or Gemini, or even to contrast these results with newer versions of ChatGPT (GPT-4o at the time of this writing). This can help to better understand the scope of each one's potential, as well as their particularities when writing both summary and argumentative texts. Secondly, given the results obtained with two very different texts, exploring the performance of AI in the writing of other textual typologies and genres could be valuable.

Finally, increasing the number of participants and incorporating other educational levels and contexts would provide a broader understanding of the findings, enabling analyses based on variables such as student age or gender. Addressing these aspects would provide a more robust picture of future teachers' knowledge about the formative potential of generative AI in language learning and improving writing skills.

Acknowledgements

We would like to thank the participants for their collaboration in this investigation.

Disclosure statement

The authors report there are no competing interests to declare.

Funding

This work was supported by the Ministry of Education, Culture and Sports of Spain under Grant numbers: FPU20/02375, FPU19/03857; the Regional Government of Castilla-La Mancha and the European Social Fund Plus (EFS+) under Grant number: 2023-PREJCCM-000054; and University of Castilla-La Mancha under Grant number: 2022-GRIN-34039

ORCID

Maria Navío-Inglés http://orcid.org/0009-0006-9127-4876
Sergio Tirado-Olivares http://orcid.org/0000-0002-8557-5115

Javier del Olmo-Muñoz http://orcid.org/0000-0001-8754-0648
Jesús Guzmán Mora http://orcid.org/0000-0001-5687-0169

References

Álvarez, I. A. (2004). Evaluación y calificación de resúmenes de textos expositivos en el aula de ILE/IFE: La guía "BABAR". *Ibérica, Revista de la Asociación Europea de Lenguas Para Fines Específicos*, (*8*), 81–99.

Bansal, H., & Khan, R. (2018). A review paper on human computer interaction. *International Journal of Advanced Research in Computer Science and Software Engineering*, *8*(4), 53. https://doi.org/10.23956/ijarcsse.v8i4.630

Barrot, J. S. (2024). ChatGPT as a language learning tool: An emerging technology report. *Technology, Knowledge and Learning*, *29*(2), 1151–1156. https://doi.org/10.1007/s10758-023-09711-4

Budzianowski, P., & Vulić, I. (2019). Hello, It's GPT-2-how can I help you? Towards the use of pretrained language models for task-oriented dialogue systems [Paper presentation]. In A. Birch, A. Finch, H. Hayashi, I. Konstas, T. Luong, G. Neubig, Y. Oda, & K. Sudoh (Eds.). *Proceedings of the 3rd Workshop on Neural Generation and Translation* (pp. 15–22). Association for Computational Linguistics. https://doi.org/10.18653/v1/D19-5602

Cassany, D. (1999). *Construir la escritura*. Paidós.

Chang, Y., Wang, X., Wang, J., Wu, Y., Yang, L., Zhu, K., Chen, H., Yi, X., Wang, C., Wang, Y., Ye, W., Zhang, Y., Chang, Y., Yu, P. S., Yang, Q., & Xie, X. (2024). A survey on evaluation of large language models. *ACM Transactions on Intelligent Systems and Technology*, *15*(3), 1–45. https://doi.org/10.1145/3641289

Cong-Lem, N., Soyoof, A., & Tsering, D. (2024). A systematic review of the limitations and associated opportunities of ChatGPT. *International Journal of Human–Computer Interaction*, 1–16. https://doi.org/10.1080/10447318.2024.2344142

Cunningham-Nelson, S., Boles, W., Trouton, L., & Margerison, E. (2019). A review of chatbots in education: Practical steps forward In *30th annual conference for the Australasian association for engineering education (AAEE 2019): Educators becoming agents of change: Innovate, integrate, motivate* (pp. 299–306). Engineers Australia.

Dale, R. (2021). GPT-3: What's it good for? *Natural Language Engineering*, *27*(1), 113–118. https://doi.org/10.1017/S1351324920000601

de Winter, J. C. (2024). Can ChatGPT pass high school exams on English language comprehension? *International Journal of Artificial Intelligence in Education*, *34*(3), 915–930. https://doi.org/10.1007/s40593-023-00372-z

Ennals, R. (1982). History teaching and artificial intelligence. *Teaching History*, (33), 3–5.

Fernández Merino, M. (2015). La expresión escrita. In E. Martínez Carro, M. Simón Parra, M. García Sánchez, M. Fernández Merino, & M. Ortiz Canseco (Eds.), *Didáctica de la Lengua Española en Educación Primaria* (pp. 139–166). UNIR Editorial.

Field, A. (2009). *Discovering statistics using SPSS*. Sage Publications.

Gao, C. A., Howard, F. M., Markov, N. S., Dyer, E. C., Ramesh, S., Luo, Y., & Pearson, A. T. (2023). Comparing scientific abstracts generated by ChatGPT to real abstracts with detectors and blinded human reviewers. *NPJ Digital Medicine*, *6*(1), 75. https://doi.org/10.1038/s41746-023-00819-6

Godwin-Jones, R. (2022). Partnering with AI: Intelligent writing assistance and instructed language learning. *Language Learning & Technology*, *26*(2), 5–24. 10125/73474

Graham, S. (2018). Instructional feedback in writing. In A. A. Lipnevich, & J. K. Smith (Eds.), *The Cambridge handbook of instructional feedback* (pp. 145–168). Cambridge University Press. https://doi.org/10.1017/9781316832134.009

Guo, B., Zhang, X., Wang, Z., Jiang, M., Nie, J., Ding, Y., Yue, J., Wu, Y. (2023). How close is ChatGPT to human experts? Comparison corpus, evaluation, and detection. ArXiv:2301.07597. https://doi.org/10.48550/arXiv.2301.07597

Herbold, S., Hautli-Janisz, A., Heuer, U., Kikteva, Z., & Trautsch, A. (2023). A large-scale comparison of human-written versus ChatGPT-generated essays. *Scientific Reports*, *13*(1), 18617. https://doi.org/10.1038/s41598-023-45644-9

Hirschberg, J., & Manning, C. D. (2015). Advances in natural language processing. *Science (New York, N.Y.)*, *349*(6245), 261–266. https://doi.org/10.1126/science.aaa8685

Huang, J., & Tan, M. (2023). The role of ChatGPT in scientific communication: Writing better scientific review articles. *American Journal of Cancer Research*, *13*(4), 1148–1154.

Hwang, G.-J., & Chang, C.-Y. J. I. L. E. (2023). A review of opportunities and challenges of chatbots in education. *Interactive Learning Environments*, *31*(7), 4099–4112. https://doi.org/10.1080/10494820.2021.1952615

Kasneci, E., Sessler, K., Küchemann, S., Bannert, M., Dementieva, D., Fischer, F., Gasser, U., Groh, G., Günnemann, S., Hüllermeier, E., Krusche, S., Kutyniok, G., Michaeli, T., Nerdel, C., Pfeffer, J., Poquet, O., Sailer, M., Schmidt, A., Seidel, T., … Kasneci, G. (2023). ChatGPT for good? On opportunities and challenges of large language models for education. *Learning and Individual Differences*, *103*, 102274. https://doi.org/10.1016/j.lindif.2023.102274

Kim, H.-S., Cha, Y., & Kim, N.-Y. (2020). Impact of mobile interactions with AI on writing performance. *Modern English Education*, *21*(2), 1–13. https://doi.org/10.18095/meeso.2020.21.2.1

Kulik, J. A., & Fletcher, J. D. (2016). Effectiveness of intelligent tutoring systems: A meta-analytic review. *Review of Educational Research*, *86*(1), 42–78. https://doi.org/10.3102/0034654315581420

Lim, W. M., Gunasekara, A., Pallant, J. L., Pallant, J. I., & Pechenkina, E. (2023). Generative AI and the future of education: Ragnarök or reformation? A paradoxical perspective from management educators. *The International Journal of Management Education*, *21*(2), 100790. https://doi.org/10.1016/j.ijme.2023.100790

Lo, C. K. (2023). What is the impact of ChatGPT on education? A rapid review of the literature. *Education Sciences*, *13*(4), 410. https://doi.org/10.3390/educsci13040410

Lund, B. D., & Wang, T. (2023). Chatting about ChatGPT: How may AI and GPT impact academia and libraries? *Library Hi Tech News*, *40*(3), 26–29. https://doi.org/10.1108/LHTN-01-2023-0009

Martínez-Huamán, E. L., Bellido Miranda, A., Félix Benites, E. D., & García Rivas Plata, C. E. (2022). Elaboración y validación de una rúbrica para medir competencias de comunicación escrita. *Revista Universidad y Sociedad*, *14*(S5), 490–505.

Mitrović, S., Andreoletti, D., & Ayoub, O. (2023). ChatGPT or human? Detect and explain. Explaining decisions of machine learning model for detecting short ChatGPT-generated text. *Ed*ArXiv. https://doi.org/10.48550/arXiv.2301.13852

Navarro-Guzmán, C., & Casero-Martínez, A. (2012). Análisis de las diferencias de género en la elección de estudios universitarios. *Estudios Sobre Educacion*, *22*, 115–132. https://doi.org/10.15581/004.22.2075

Okonkwo, C. W., & Ade-Ibijola, A. (2021). Chatbots applications in education: A systematic review. *Computers and Education: Artificial Intelligence*, *2*, 100033. https://doi.org/10.1016/j.caeai.2021.100033

Pavlik, J. V. (2023). Collaborating with ChatGPT: Considering the implications of generative artificial intelligence for journalism and media education. *Journalism & Mass Communication Educator*, *78*(1), 84–93. https://doi.org/10.1177/10776958221149577

Pelletier, K., McCormack, M., Muscanell, N., Reeves, J., Robert, J., & Arbino, N. (2024). *2024 EDUCAUSE Horizon Report,* Teaching and Learning Edition. Educause.

Polak, S., Schiavo, G., & Zancanaro, M. (2022). Teachers' Perspective on Artificial Intelligence Education: An Initial Investigation [Paper presentation]. In *Extended Abstracts of the 2022 CHI Conference on Human Factors in Computing Systems (CHI EA '22)* (pp. 1–7). Association for Computing Machinery. https://doi.org/10.1145/3491101.3519866

Radford, A., Narasimhan, K., Salimans, T., & Sutskever, I. (2018). Improving language understanding by generative pre-training. Preprint.

Shawar, B. A., & Atwell, E. (2007). Chatbots: Are they really useful? *Journal for Language Technology and Computational Linguistics, 22*(1), 29–49. https://doi.org/10.21248/jlcl.22.2007.88

Simón Parra, M. (2015). La enseñanza de la lectura y la escritura en Primaria: La lectoescritura In E. Martínez Carro, M. Simón Parra, M. García Sánchez, M. Fernández Merino, & M. Ortiz Canseco (Eds.), *Didáctica de la Lengua Española en Educación Primaria* (pp. 45–64). UNIR Editorial.

Song, C., & Song, Y. (2023). Enhancing academic writing skills and motivation: Assessing the efficacy of ChatGPT in AI-assisted language learning for EFL students. *Frontiers in Psychology, 14*, 1260843. https://doi.org/10.3389/fpsyg.2023.1260843

Stevenson, M. (2016). A critical interpretative synthesis: The integration of Automated Writing Evaluation into classroom writing instruction. *Computers and Composition, 42*, 1–16. https://doi.org/10.1016/j.compcom.2016.05.001

Tegos, S., Demetriadis, S., & Tsiatsos, T. (2014). A configurable conversational agent to trigger students' productive dialogue: A pilot study in the call domain. *International Journal of Artificial Intelligence in Education, 24*(1), 62–91. https://doi.org/10.1007/s40593-013-0007-3

Tirado-Olivares, S., Navío-Inglés, M., O'Connor-Jiménez, P., & Cózar-Gutiérrez, R. (2023). From human to machine: Investigating the effectiveness of the conversational AI ChatGPT in historical thinking. *Education Sciences, 13*(8), 803. https://doi.org/10.3390/educsci13080803

Williams, C., & Beam, S. (2019). Technology and writing: Review of research. *Computers & Education, 128*, 227–242. https://doi.org/10.1016/j.compedu.2018.09.024

Wilson, J., & Czik, A. (2016). Automated essay evaluation software in English Language Arts classrooms: Effects on teacher feedback, student motivation, and writing quality. *Computers & Education, 100*, 94–109. https://doi.org/10.1016/j.compedu.2016.05.004

World Economic Forum. (2024). *Shaping the future of learning: The role of AI in education 4.0.*

Yazdani, M., & Lawler, R. W. (1986). Artificial intelligence and education: An overview. *Instructional Science, 14*(3-4), 197–206. https://doi.org/10.1007/BF00051820

Zhang, K., & Aslan, A. B. (2021). AI technologies for education: Recent research & future directions. *Computers and Education: Artificial Intelligence, 2*, 100025. https://doi.org/10.1016/j.caeai.2021.100025

Zhang, P., & Tur, G. (2023). A systematic review of ChatGPT use in K-12 education. *European Journal of Education, 59*(2), e12599. https://doi.org/10.1111/ejed.12599

Appendix 1. Activities evaluated by the participants

Summary

Pre-service teacher	This text talks about the European Commission's proposal "One Hundred Smart and Climate-Neutral Cities by 2030." The text presents the imbalance in energy use and CO_2 emissions on the planet, with European countries consuming more than half of the world's energy, especially in urban populations. This proposal, which has selected 100 cities (7 of them Spanish), asks to present a "climate contract" with realistic goals to achieve climate neutrality.
ChatGPT	The article reports on the European Commission's initiative to support the transition toward climate neutrality in 100 cities through a science and innovation program in which seven Spanish cities will participate. Each city will have to present a "climate contract" with specific objectives and transformative projects, and an investment of between 10,000 and 30,000 euros per inhabitant is expected from public and private funds. The aim is to accelerate the transition to climate neutrality across cities and reduce the gap between large cities and the rest of the country.

Argumentative text

Pre-service teacher	I don't think this goal will be achieved, since emissions and energy use do not depend as much on citizens, but on large companies, which are the ones that really drive these numbers up. Companies are private, and they handle enormous amounts of money, so a reduction in their performance or a renovation towards more sustainable methods could result in a relocation of these companies to other countries with more lenient regulations. We must consider that penalties (or non-penalties) can be paid or ignored, with no consequences in terms of sustainability. If the companies were expropriated and the state took over ensuring compliance with these regulations, then this could be achieved.
ChatGPT	Making one hundred European cities climate neutral by 2030 is an ambitious and challenging goal. While it is possible that some of the cities selected for the program may be able to achieve climate neutrality by the proposed timeframe, it is unlikely that all will achieve it due to differences in the conditions and resources of each city. In addition, some cities may experience delays due to technical, economic or political problems. However, the initiative is important because it helps to raise awareness of the need to take action to combat climate change and promote urban sustainability. Furthermore, the program can encourage innovation and the development of sustainable technologies and practices and can serve as a model for other cities. In summary, although the goal of one hundred climate-neutral cities by 2030 is unlikely to be achieved, the initiative is valuable for its impact on awareness and innovation.

Summary

Pre-service teacher	Este texto nos habla acerca de la propuesta de la Comisión Europea "Cien ciudades inteligentes y climáticamente neutras de aquí a 2030". El texto nos presenta el desequilibrio del uso de energía y emisiones de CO2 del planeta, siendo los países europeos los que consumen más de la mitad de energía del mundo, especialmente en las poblaciones urbanas. Esta propuesta, que ha seleccionado 100 ciudades (7 de ellas españolas) pide presentar un "contrato climático" con objetivos realistas para alcanzar la neutralidad climática.
ChatGPT	El artículo informa sobre la iniciativa de la Comisión Europea de apoyar la transición hacia la neutralidad climática en 100 ciudades a través de un programa de ciencia e innovación en el que participarán siete ciudades españolas. Cada ciudad deberá presentar un "contrato climático" con objetivos específicos y proyectos transformadores, y se espera una inversión de entre 10,000 y 30,000 euros por habitante, proveniente de fondos públicos y privados. El objetivo es acelerar la transición hacia la neutralidad climática a través de las ciudades y reducir la brecha entre las grandes ciudades y el resto del país.

Argumentative text

Pre-service teacher	Creo que no se alcanzará este objetivo, ya que las emisiones y uso de energía no dependen tanto de los ciudadanos, sino de las grandes empresas que son las que realmente engrosan estas cifras. Las empresas son de ámbito privado, y mueven cantidades ingentes de dinero, con lo cual una reducción de su rendimiento o renovación hacia métodos más sostenibles podría suponer un traslado de estas empresas a otros países con normativas más laxas. También hemos de tener en cuenta que las sanciones (o no sanciones) pueden ser pagadas o ignoradas, sin consecuencias en el ámbito de la sostenibilidad. Si las empresas fueran expropiadas y el estado pasara a velar por el cumplimiento de estas normas, entonces sí se podría alcanzar.
ChatGPT	Lograr que cien ciudades europeas sean climáticamente neutras para 2030 es un objetivo ambicioso y desafiante. Si bien es posible que algunas de las ciudades seleccionadas para el programa puedan lograr la neutralidad climática en el plazo previsto, es poco probable que todas lo consigan debido a las diferencias en las condiciones y recursos de cada ciudad. Además, es posible que algunas ciudades experimenten retrasos debido a problemas técnicos, económicos o políticos. Sin embargo, la iniciativa es importante porque contribuye a aumentar la conciencia sobre la necesidad de adoptar medidas para combatir el cambio climático y promover la sostenibilidad urbana. Además, el programa puede fomentar la innovación y el desarrollo de tecnologías y prácticas sostenibles, y puede servir de modelo para otras ciudades. En resumen, aunque es poco probable que se logre el objetivo de cien ciudades climáticamente neutras para 2030, la iniciativa es valiosa por su impacto en la conciencia y la innovación.

ChatGPT-Produced Content as a Resource in the Language Education Classroom: A Guiding Hand

Rod Case and Leping Liu

ABSTRACT
While there is much in teacher education which examines the perceptions of preservice teacher to the recent introduction of ChatGPT. This study examines preservice teachers' appraisals of ChatGPT-produced text. Using a quasi-experimental within--subject design with 30 participants, Chi-Square tests examined appraisals under three conditions. Results indicated that appraisal of ChatGPT-produced text was higher when prepared by the instructor among students who demonstrated an understanding of the pedagogical content versus those who did not. Appraisals were also sensitive to where ChatGPT-produced text was placed in the assignment, favoring use of ChatGPT at beginning of the assignment versus in the middle. A discussion of implications for using ChatGPT-produced text is included.

Introduction

Since the introduction of ChatGPT, a chatbot that uses artificial intelligence (AI), educators and the larger public sector have both praised and questioned its functionality (e.g., Javier & Moorhouse, 2024; Moorhouse, 2024; Moorhouse & Kohnke, 2024; Yang & Appleget, 2024). Within teacher education research, ChatGPT is lauded for its ability to quickly produce lessons (e.g., Farrokhnia et al., 2024), classroom exercises, and assessments (Li et al., 2024; van den Berg & Du Plessis, 2023). Further, its use with preservice teachers is linked to gains in critical thinking skills (Li et al., 2024). Enthusiasm for these early findings into its potential as an instructional tool has inspired others to provide highly detailed descriptions of ChatGPT-generated lesson plans, materials and assessments that serve as instructional resources for teachers (e.g., Kohnke et al., 2023; Kostka & Toncelli, 2023).

Beyond education, ChatGPT has demonstrated its prowess across multiple fields.Researchers have confirmed ChatGPT is capable of analyzing complex texts, creating sound arguments, and passing exams across disparate fields such as medicine (Gilson et al., 2022; Huh, 2023), physics/

engineering (Yeadon et al., 2023), and law (Katz et al., 2023). In the fields of literature and philosophy, Elkins and Chun (2020) note that it provides insightful and nuanced arguments by relying on a strong command of form and rhetoric. However, they also argue that is also lacks a human-driven type of common sense and conclude that while its abilities are impressive it falls short of human writers.

Despite these advances, teacher educators have not explored the potential of ChatGPT-produced texts in the classroom. Early evidence studies focused on preservice teachers' perceptions of ChatGPT (e.g., Javier & Moorhouse, 2024; Moorhouse, 2024; Moorhouse & Kohnke, 2024; Yang & Appleget, 2024) or its potential risks, such as facilitating academic plagiarism due to its ability to produce text indistinguishable from human writing (Khalaf, 2024). However, less is known about how ChatGPT-produced text can support pedagogical content learning in teacher education that activities which incorporate the use of ChatGPT build a deeper understanding of course content among preservice teachers than activities which do not, particularly when teacher educators structure the prompts given ChatGPT.

Emerging evidence (Case & Liu, 2024, under review) suggests that incorporating ChatGPT into instructional tasks can enhance preservice teachers' understanding of pedagogical content. Case and Liu (2024, under review) showed that students benefited more when they critiqued a ChatGPT-produced lesson prepared by the teacher, versus prompts that they created themselves. Furthermore, ChatGPT-produced text was most effective when introduced at the beginning of the instructional task and prompted by the instructor, rather than as a follow-up and prompted by the student. The authors concluded that this was largely due to the fact that the instructor had a deeper knowledge of the course content than the students, allowing him to prompt ChatGPT with more knowledgeable prompts and produce higher quality responses. The researchers called for greater research as to why placing it at the initial position in the task was significant, confirming research which suggests that the quality of the prompt, which is dependent upon an understanding of how ChatGPT constructs responses and knowledge of the content area, is a strong predictor of the accuracy of the response (Gilson et al., 2022).

This research, which was conducted in 2024, builds on work by Case and Liu (2024, under review). The purpose of this study is to explore how language teacher educators use ChatGPT-produced texts as a resource to explore pedagogical content without ignoring questions about its ability to provide insights into a field that is driven by human experience. To do this, a content analysis, a research method which involves the coding of texts into the themes or, in this case, concepts, in order to conduct a quantitative analysis (Weber, 1990), of students' work was completed over the course of two semesters. The analysis examined the extent to which preservice teachers' appraisals of ChatGPT-produced text were associated with their understanding of the course content, positioning the use of ChatGPT-produced text at the beginning and the middle of the instructional sequences.

Literature review

ChatGPT in language teacher education

Work in language teacher education (LTE) has focused on linking perceptions of ChatGPT to preservice teachers' willingness to use it in instructional practice. While limited in their scope, these studies are often classroom-based accounts that identify the extent to which the preservice teachers' attitudes about ChatGPT, experience with using it, and knowledge of its functions are reliable indicators of their likelihood of using it (e.g., Javier & Moorhouse, 2024; Moorhouse, 2024; Moorhouse & Kohnke, 2024; Yang & Appleget, 2024). Giving preservice teachers the opportunity to use ChatGPT to plan instruction and also guide students as they use ChatGPT in the classroom is key, but, while it is tempting to assume that preservice teachers already have detailed knowledge of ChatGPT, many do not. Preservice teachers who have not had the opportunity to use it at home, may not feel as confident in using it to create lessons or classroom materials as those who have (Moorhouse, 2024).

The benefits of preservice teachers using ChatGPT are beginning to emerge. While many have documented how it frees teachers from routine tasks such as creating lessons, worksheets, and assessments (e.g., Li et al., 2024; van den Berg & Du Plessis, 2023), more interesting is research that suggests that it can enhance critical thinking skills (Li et al., 2024; van den Berg & Du Plessis, 2023). Li et al. (2024), for instance, found that preservice teachers who had interacted with ChatGPT, labeled as the "Human-Machine" group, demonstrated higher levels of critical thinking on post-test measures than preservice teachers who had only interacted with the instructor, labeled the "Human-Human" group. Li et al. (2024) drew on work by Rusandi et al. (2023) and Ciechanowski et al. (2019) to argue that the reason for the increase in critical thinking might be attributable to the fact that preservice teachers often checked ChatGPT's work against outside sources.

Still, allowing students to use ChatGPT in the classroom without guidance is not recommended. Building on specific work by Li et al. (2024) and others more broadly (e.g., Cooper, 2023; Farrokhnia et al., 2024; Skrabut, 2023; van den Berg & Du Plessis, 2023), Jeon and Lee (2023) found that few teachers advocated the practice of allowing students to experiment with ChatGPT without close supervision. Most teachers called for a mix of using ChatGPT to assist in lesson planning and then closely supervising students during its use. While helpful, these researchers have not examined how preservice teachers learn to navigate the affordances and constraints of ChatGPT-produced lessons, assessment and content while they are still learning to teach.

The affordances and constraints of ChatGPT-produced text

To date, research into the capabilities of ChatGPT to produce academic texts or classroom materials appropriate for the preservice teachers pursuing teacher licensure has been limited to explorations of preservice or inservice teachers' perceptions of ChatGPT's instructional prowess (e.g., Javier & Moorhouse, 2024; Moorhouse, 2024; Moorhouse & Kohnke, 2024; Yang & Appleget, 2024). This scholarship often connects teachers' perceptions of ChatGPT to their predictions of how ChatGPT might perform in the classroom. While valuable, it often lacks an exploration of the nature and quality of ChatGPT and is completed with a limited number of examples that were not subjected to experimental conditions.

In response to this gap in the research, the review below details existing research into the nature of ChatGPT-produced texts. While the research is drawn from fields outside of teacher education (e.g., medicine, Gilson et al. (2022), Huh (2023), physics/engineering, Yeadon et al. (2023), literature/philosophy, Elkins and Chun (2020) and law Katz et al. (2023), there is much that can be inferred in building an introductory understanding of ChatGPT-produced text for the teacher educator.

One strand of this research explores ChatGPT's performance on various standardized exams as an indicator of its capability to process content accurately. While Huh (2023) found that ChatGPT did not outperform humans on a standardized test of parasitology that included both multiple choice and written responses, Huh (2023) also noted that one possible explanation for the lower scores might be that ChatGPT's inability to interpret tables and images competently. Gilson et al. (2022) accounted for these limitations in a measure of ChatGPT's medical knowledge as demonstrated on its performance on the United States Medical Exam. Questions that contained images or tables were removed, and sample questions in each prompt were added. Results showed performance on the first level of the exam to be comparable to third-year medical students but declining performance on the remaining two levels. ChatGPT-produced writing samples and evidenced highly logical explanations throughout.

Other research corroborates work by Huh (2023) and Gilson et al. (2022), confirming ChatGPT's capabilities to integrate complex content into logical well-written text (e.g., Katz et al., 2023; Yeadon et al., 2023;

Zhai, 2022). Findings from Katz et al. (2023), for instance, measured performance on the Universal Bar Examination (UBE) and its three components: (1) the multistate bar exam (MBE), multistate essay exam (MEE), and multistate performance test (MPT). ChatGPT-4 outperformed the pass rate of law students on the MBE, but, more specific to the question of its capabilities to create documents which demonstrate high levels of analytical thought, ChatGPT-4 outperformed previous iterations of ChatGPT on the MEE. Its essays demonstrated the ability to analyze complex legal issues which require the writer to deduce answers through the use of entailment and competently connect knowledge of the law to the issue of interest.

In a turn from exploring the capabilities of ChatGPT on standardized tests in the sciences, Elkins and Chun (2020) delved into ChatGPT's performance on examining literature and philosophy. Drawing on their experiences as professors of literature and philosophy, they examined ChatGPT's ability to form arguments, Elkins and Chun (2020) found that while ChatGPT described the insights that drive works of philosophy by Plato and Nietzsche with humor, irony and playfulness, they argued that without "judicious" selection of its work ChatGPT would probably not pass a writer's Turing Test. In other words, it could not produce a text that is indistinguishable from one created by a human. Its writing is inconsistent. While it readily emulates rhetorical form and explore complex philosophical arguments, it also lacks what they described as "commonsense and foundational knowledge" (p. 12) which is typically present in texts created by humans. While findings from Elkins and Chun (2020) stop short of proposing that ChatGPT could emulate human writing, they leave open the possibility for exploration of its potential as interesting source of writing and knowledge which students could learn from.

Theoretical framework

According to Shabani (2016), there is common agreement that three themes drive Vygotsky (1986) work: (a) a close examination of individual development to understand intellectual growth, (b) the claim that cognitive growth is rooted in social experience, and (c) a focus on the mediated nature of learning. Of the three, the third is most closely related to teacher education, as it speaks to the central role of mediation and the Zone of Proximal Development (ZPD) in classroom instruction. Johnson and Golombek (2020) sociocultural framework builds on Vygotsky's (1986) work and details eight propositions intended to guide language teacher educators in their instruction of preservice teachers. Three concepts central to Johnson and Golombek (2020) framework, mediation, everyday concept and academic concept, are examined below.

Mediation is the driving force for all instruction and highlights the central role that the teacher educator plays as the more knowledgeable other in interactions with preservice teachers. The teacher educator is tasked with creating mediational spaces for preservice teachers in which they are encouraged to "play/step" into becoming teachers. Johnson and Golombek (2020) call on teacher educators to establish these spaces as "safe-zones" for trying out new ideas that their preservice teachers are not yet ready to carry out in the classroom without assistance. Ideally, preservice teachers should feel free to reflect on and critique their still-emerging ideas about pedagogical content. Course curriculum is structured around goal-directed activities which can include practicum, written essays, lesson planning or various kinds of discussion activities (e.g., Case & Liu, 2024, under review).

Next, learning for preservice teachers begins as an everyday concept. Everyday concepts emerge from experiences both within and outside of school settings. While preservice teachers' ideas about language, language teaching, and technology, which form from these experiences are often flawed, superficial, or unanalyzed, they are not to be dismissed or regarded as a deficit (Johnson & Golombek, 2020). Rather, they are the building blocks for movement toward an academic concept.

Johnson and Golombek (2020) described academic concepts as representing "systematic and generalizable knowledge of entities and phenomenon in the world" (p. 122). Unlike everyday concepts, academic concepts are systematically formed and emerge from the kinds of structured learning experiences emerge with formal instruction (Lantolf & Minakova, 2021). Preservice teachers who have knowledge of pedagogical content as an academic concept are able to create lessons and make judgements about their teaching that can be generalized across different contexts.

Need for research

How can teacher education research into the use of ChatGPT and the broader multidisciplinary exploration of the nature of ChatGPT-produced text inform examinations of ChatGPT in LTE? Teacher education research suggests that ChatGPT has the potential to increase critical thinking (Li et al., 2024), provided there are ample opportunities to build background experiences with using ChatGPT (Moorhouse, 2024). Research which explores the use of ChatGPT-produced texts in teacher education has not been forthcoming despite its potential to synthesizing large amounts of data and creating cogent, logical explanations and analyses in fields as diverse as medicine (Gilson et al., 2022; Huh, 2023), physics/engineering (Yeadon et al., 2023), literature/philosophy (Elkins & Chun, 2020) and law (Katz et al., 2023), suggesting that ChatGPT is able to form generalizable knowledge that can be applied to a variety of circumstances, a hallmark of an academic concept. Building on work by Case and Liu (2024, under review), this study fills that gap in the research by exploring extent to which preservice teachers' appraisals of ChatGPT-produced texts were associated with the presence of academic concepts in their work.

Research questions

The learning outcome in this study was measured by whether or not students included academic concepts in their course work. In order to operationalize the measurement of academic concepts, two measurement criteria inferred from Johnson and Golombek (2020), definition and application, were developed. The third criteria informed by research on the use of prompts in ChatGPT-produced texts (Huh, 2023) was technical concerns. Technical concerns were identified when students expressed concerns with the results of their prompts when using ChatGPT.

Measurement of students' appraisals of ChatGPT-produced text were also conducted. These were sorted into three categories: rejected, ambivalent, and accepted. Research question one provided an overall measurement of the students' appraisals of their readings of ChatGPT-produced text in terms of *definition*, *application* and *technical concerns*. Research question two measured the extent to which students' learning outcomes from three different instructional sequences (explored more fully below) were associated with their appraisal of definition, application and technical concerns.

The organization of the assignments varied along two elements. First, assignments differed according to whether the instructor or the students prompted ChatGPT with directions. In the second element, the placement of ChatGPT-produced text was varied. ChatGPT-produced text was introduced at one of three points in the instructional task. Each one of these variations was called an instructional sequence. In sequence one, the instructor provided the ChatGPT-produced text in the middle of the instructional task. In sequence two, the teacher educator included the ChatGPT-produced text at the beginning of the instructional task, and, finally, in sequence three, the instructor added ChatGPT-produced text at the beginning of the instructional task. Utilizing the parameters describe above, this study asked two research questions:

1. Are students' learning outcomes from each instructional sequence associated with the overall appraisals one each type of information that they identified from the ChatGPT-produced text: (a) definition, (b) application, and (c) technical concerns?
2. Are students' learning outcomes from each instructional sequence associated with their appraisals (rejected, ambivalent, and accepted)

on each type of information that they identified from ChatGPT-produced text?

Methodology

Design

A quasi-experimental within-subject design was adopted in this study (Nicolaidou et al., 2023) with a nonrandomized sample of preservice teachers from an existing language teacher education class. The use of ChatGPT was integrated into the three instructional sequences with all students participating in the same course. Students' learning outcomes were examined in association with their appraisals of each type of ChatGPT-produced text that they identified during the course.

Chi-Square (χ^2) tests were used for the data analysis. To determine the appropriate sample size, a priori power analysis was performed with G*Power 3.1.9.4. The α level was set at .05, and statistical power at .8 (Williamson, 2024). Consistent with contemporary literature (Liu, 2023), four effect size values were chosen: (.5), (.55), (.6), and (.65). The resulting minimum sample sizes were 39, 32, 27, and 23 for two by three (χ^2) tests, and 32, 26, 22, and 19 for two by two (χ^2) tests, respectively. The sample size of this study ($N = 30$) was in the appropriate range, given the expected effect size.

Participants and data sample

Thirty students from a western state university in the United States enrolled in a language teacher education course taught during the fall of 2023 and again in the spring of 2024 participated in this study. Ten were from the fall class, three males and seven females. Twenty from the spring class, six males and fourteen females. They were in their junior or senior years majoring English, Spanish, social studies, mathematics and science. The data sample for this study were the three written-assignments from each of the 30 participants completed in the three instructional sequences, resulting in a total of 90 assignments.

The course

The 16-week course was required for all juniors and seniors seeking teaching licensure. Students completed a total of seven written assignments, six discussion posts and two lesson plans. Because the course was online and asynchronous, detailed written instructions and instructor-created videos accompanied the weekly assignments. The content of the course was drawn from contemporary articles and research on language teaching and learning and introduced students to six academic concepts. The first four, funds of knowledge (de Souza, 2017; Moll, 2019), the deficit perspective (de Souza, 2017), Consejos (Goldsmith & Kurpius, 2018) and academic language (Zwiers, 2014), prepared students with foundational ideas about language instruction. The remaining two academic concepts included translanguaging (Solorza et al., 2023) and schema. While assignments varied in length and complexity, all assignments required students to demonstrate knowledge of the selected academic concept, by both expressing knowledge and use of its definition and exploring its application. This study focused on the learning activities of developing and using three academic concepts: consejos, schema, and translanguaging.

Procedures

Following Institutional Review Board approval, data collection and analysis began. Content coding of students' assignments was done to examine learning outcomes. ChatGPT-produced texts, prompted by either the instructor or the students themselves, were integrated into three instructional sequences across the three activities described below (Table 1). A description of each sequence follows.

In sequence one, the introduction of ChatGPT-produced text was prepared by the instructor and placed in the middle of the first learning activity (Table 1). This particular sequence was conducted over two weeks. In the first week, the students completed a response to Solorza's (2023) description and application of consejos (Goldsmith & Kurpius, 2018). Two weeks later, the instructor used ChatGPT to create a response to the week-one assignment. Next, the students read ChatGPT's essay and compared it with the essay they created in week one, critiquing ChatGPT's use of consejos (Goldsmith & Kurpius, 2018) in terms of the two operationalized measures of academic concept, definition and application.

Table 1. Sequences of using ChatGPT-information in learning.

Learning in:	Step1	Step 2	Step 3	Step 4
Sequence 1	Student completes first essay on consejos	***Instructor-prompted ChatGPT text is given to students***	Students compare their essay from step one with ChatGPT text from step two.	Final essay formulated around the selected academic concept
Sequence 2	***Student-prompted ChatGPT text***	Student review & identify ChatGPT text	Student essay	Final essay formulated around the selected academic concept
Sequence 3	***Instructor-prompted ChatGPT text***	Student review & identify ChatGPT text	Student written essay	Final essay formulated around the selected academic concept

Sequence two used student-prompted text and was introduced at the beginning of the instructional task. The task asked the students to use ChatGPT to create a lesson for their particular content area to apply an academic concept. They were directed to set the number of multilingual students in their class at 20%, indicate the grade level, the content area, the length of the lesson and ensure that the ChatGPT demonstrated the use of schema. Students were not given additional information such as the value of using multiple prompts or the limitations of ChatGPT to interpret tables or images. This decision provided data on their facility with ChatGPT absent formal instruction. The lesson required them to write a brief essay about the results of their efforts at creating a lesson using ChatGPT and critique its ability to explore the use of schema, the academic concept in a lesson plan.

In sequence three, the use of ChatGPT was set at the beginning of the instructional task and instructor-prompted. Translanguaging (Solorza et al., 2023) was the academic concept. The instructor entered similar parameters into ChatGPT described in sequence two. As in sequence two, images and tables were avoided. Also, multiple prompts were used to ensure that the final lesson had elements of an academic concept that students would be able to identify. Finally, as with sequences one and two, students critiqued the extent to which ChatGPT's use of translanguaging reflected an academic concept.

Content coding and variables

The data sample consisted of 90 assignments from the 30 students. The content of each assignment was examined. Learning outcomes, students-identified ChatGPT-produced text, and students' appraisal of the ChatGPT-produced texts were coded as described below.

Learning outcome

To facilitate the coding of the students' work, academic concept was operationalized by focusing on the students' abilities to define and apply the selected academic concept. Based upon a close reading of Johnson and Golombek (2020), an academic concept was present in a text when there was evidence of a definition of the pedagogical concept and an application. A definition required the students to "demonstrate systematic and generalizable knowledge of the academic concept" (Johnson & Golombek, 2020, p. 122). To meet this criterion, the work should demonstrate an understanding of internal components and structure of the academic concept. For example, the assignment might include quotes, related examples which define the academic concept in the students' own words.

The second criterion, application, required students to connect "the academic concept to personal academic activities or real-world experience"(Johnson & Golombek, 2020, p. 122). To meet this criterion, the student should describe or interpret how effectively a lesson or instructional activity communicates the use of an academic concept. Students may relate their thinking about instructional activity from their own experience as learners, describe an experience from a practicum or classroom observation, or explore an instructional activity from the week's reading. For each assignment, content coding was conducted for the presence of definition and application. When both definition and application were present, a code of (1) was given; if not, a code of (0) was assigned.

Student-identified ChatGPT-produced text

In their assignments, the preservice teachers identified and critiqued the use of definition, application and technical concerns in ChatGPT-produced text. Definition and application are the operational terms used with academic concept. These terms are described below.

Definition: With respect to academic concept, the students identified the definition in ChatGPT-produced texts where fundamental knowledge, developmental context, references or relevant examples were demonstrated.

The students' writing showed an understanding of fundamental knowledge of the academic concept. This might include use of references, relevant examples and/or discussion of the definition of one of the academic concepts such as funds of knowledge (de Souza, 2017; Moll, 2019), the deficit perspective (de Souza, 2017), Consejos (Goldsmith & Kurpius, 2018) and academic language (Zwiers, 2014).

Application: Students identified and critiqued ChatGPT-produced application, according to the ChatGPT descriptions of relevant or suggested, real-world or hypothetical activities and instructional ideas.

Technical concerns: Technical concerns were identified when students expressed concerns with the results of their prompts when using ChatGPT. The most common technical concern was having to prompt ChatGPT multiple times in order to get a desired response.

Appraisal of ChatGPT-produced texts

The students also appraised the use of definition, application and technical concerns in ChatGPT-produced texts. The researchers coded the appraisals that the students identified. With respect to definition and application, the variable was coded into three categories: rejected, ambivalent, and accepted. These were coded as (1), (2), and (3), respectively:

Rejected: The students rejected the use of ChatGPT, as they found that it did not present a knowledgeable description of the academic concept after repeated attempts at prompting it.

Ambivalent: The students were ambivalent about the use of ChatGPT. ChatGPT represented a viable tool that could inform their practice as future teachers, but its future use is contingent upon their willingness to prompt ChatGPT several times in order to find a satisfactory response. Also, students were ambivalent when ChatGPT's discussion and definition of the required academic concept or application was not fully developed or had small errors in the response.

Accepted: Students identified the contents as accepted when they found that all aspects of ChatGPT's response were correct and could inform their practice as future teachers without further prompting of ChatGPT.

With respect to technical concerns, the variable was coded into two categories: concern expressed and concern not expressed, which were coded as (1) and (0), respectively. The association between learning outcome and the appraisals that the students identified in ChatGPT-produced text was examined.

Intra-rater reliability analysis

In content coding, reliability analysis is suggested to determine either the interrater reliability or the intra-rater reliability (Rourke et al., 2001; Weber, 1990, p. 15). In this study, intra-rater reliability analysis was performed.

The content coding for the four variables (academic concept, definition, application, and technical concern) in each assignment was first completed using all samples (all 90 assignments). Consistent with research from Hanselman and Liu (2021), the same researcher revisited the data to verify the reliability of the initial coding. As 15% of the sample was recommended as appropriate for the intra-rater reliability check (Landis & Koch, 1977), the researchers randomly selected and recoded 25 assignments (about 27% of the total amount of data) for the intra-rater reliability analysis. Cohen's Kappa (K) statistic was conducted to examine the level of agreement in the coding results between the two coding periods (Cohen, 1960). Values of Kappa between .40 and .59 are considered moderate. Between .60 and .79 are considered substantial, and above .80 are considered outstanding (Landis & Koch, 1977). The results of the intra-rater reliability Kappa tests on academic concept ($K = .839$, $p < .001$), definition ($K = .839$, $p < .001$), application ($K = .936$, $p < .001$), and technical concern ($K = .689$, $p < .001$) indicated that the level of agreement between the two coding periods regarding the four variables were substantial. The data from the first coding was used for data analysis.

Data analyses and results

A nonparametric analysis method Chi-Square test of independence was used for the data analyses of the study. The results are presented according to the research questions below.

Data analyses and results for research question one

In the data analysis for research question one, learning outcomes and overall appraisal from each instructional sequence was examined using Chi-Square (χ^2) tests. Three Chi-Square (χ^2) tests were conducted in each sequence: (a) learning outcome by definition, (b) learning outcome by application, and (c) learning outcome by technical concerns.

In instructional sequence one, the learning outcome was significantly associated with the students' overall appraisal of definition in ChatGPT-produced texts (χ^2 = 13.526, N=28, p = .004, effect size *Cramer's V* = .695, p = .004) but not significantly associated with students' appraisals of either application (χ^2 = 3.073, N=28, p = .215, *Cramer's V* = .331, p = .215) or technical concern(χ^2 = 1.163, N=28, p = .281, *Cramer's V* = .204, p = .281).

In sequence two, the learning outcome was significantly associated with the students' overall appraisal of definition in ChatGPT-produced texts (χ^2 = 10.383, N=27, p = .006, effect size *Cramer's V* = .620, p = .006), but not significantly associated with either application (χ^2 = 1.485, N=27, p = .476, *Cramer's V* = .235, p = .476) or technical concern (χ^2 = .667, N=27, p = .414, *Cramer's V* = .157, p = .414).

In sequence three, the learning outcome was significantly associated with the students' overall appraisal of definition in ChatGPT-produced texts (χ^2= 10.887, N=27, p = .012, effect size *Cramer's V* = .635, p = .012) and the ChatGPT-produced application (χ^2 = 17.532, N=27, p < .001, *Cramer's V* = .806, p < .001) but not significantly associated with their appraisal of technical concern (χ^2 = 1.485, N=27, p = .476, *Cramer's V* = .235, p = .476).

In summary, the students' overall appraisal of definition in ChatGPT-produced texts was associated with the learning outcome in all three sequences. The overall appraisal of application in ChatGPT-produced texts was associated with the learning outcome only in sequence three. The overall appraisal of technical concern with respect to ChatGPT-produced texts was not associated with any of the three sequences. No further tests were performed on the appraisal of technical concern.

Data analyses and results for research question two

In the data analysis for research question two, learning outcomes from each sequence were examined with Chi-Square (χ^2) tests by the specific appraisal (rejected, ambivalent, and accepted) of definition in ChatGPT-produced texts. Second, the learning outcome from sequence three was examined with Chi-Square (χ^2) tests by the specific appraisal of application in ChatGPT-produced texts. The following are the results from the Chi-Square (χ^2) tests.

Sequence one: Learning outcomes by the appraisal of definition

In sequence one, the instructor-prompted ChatGPT-produced text was included in the middle of the instructional sequence. Results indicated that the proportion of correct assignments in which the students' appraisal of definition in ChatGPT-produced texts was "accepted" waslarger than the proportion of correct assignments that were "rejected" or appraised as "ambivalent" (Table 2).

For example, the results of the third Chi-Square (χ^2) test were significant (χ^2 = 8.64, N=24, p = .003, effect size *Phi* (φ) = .60), indicating that the proportions of correct assignments (learning outcome =1) and incorrect assignments (learning outcome = 0) varied significantly between those in which definition was identified as "ambivalent" and as "accepted." In the 15 correct assignments, 9 (60%) were identified as "accepted" on definition, which was higher than "ambivalent" 6 (40%). In the 9 incorrect assignments, students did not identify any one (0%) as "accepted" but 9 (100%) identified definition as "ambivalent."

Sequence two: Learning outcomes by the appraisal of definition

In sequence two, the student-prompted ChatGPT-produced text was provided at the beginning of the instructional sequence. Results indicated that the proportion of correct assignments in which the students' appraisal of definition in ChatGPT-produced texts was "accepted" was smaller than "rejected" or appraised as "ambivalent" (Table 3).

Table 2. Chi-square comparison tests for definition in sequence 1.

GPT info-quality as identified	Learning outcomes		Chi-square results		
	0^a	1^b	χ^2	*p*	*Phi* (φ)*
	(n=12)	(n=6)			
Rejected	3 (40%)	0 (0 %)	1.80	.180	.318
Ambivalent	9 (60%)	6 (100 %)			
	(n=3)	(n=9)			
Rejected	3 (100%)	0 (0 %)	12.00	<.001	1.00
Accepted	0 (0 %)	9 (100%)			
	(n=9)	(n=15)			
Ambivalent	9 (100%)	6 (40.0%)	8.64	.003	.600
Accepted	0 (0 %)	9 (60.0%)			

Notes:

*All the *Phi* (φ) tests had the same significant level of *p* as in each of the χ^2 tests.

(1^b) Assignments that the academic concepts were correctly formulated.

(0^a) Assignments that the academic concepts were not correctly formulated.

For example, the results of the third Chi-Square (χ^2) test were significant (χ^2 = 6.008, N=23, p = .014, *Phi* (φ) = .511), indicating that the proportions of correct and incorrect assignments were significantly different between those in which the students' appraisals of definition was "ambivalent" and appraised as "accepted." In the 4 correct assignments, the students' appraisal of definition was "accepted" 1 (25%), which was smaller than the occurrences of "ambivalent" 3 (75%). In the 19 incorrect assignments, the students' appraisal of definition was accepted in 16 (60%) and "ambivalent" in 3 (40%).

Sequence three: Learning outcomes by the appraisal of definition

In sequence three, the instructor-prompted ChatGPT-produced text was provided at the beginning of instructional sequence. Results indicated that the proportion of correct assignments in which the students' appraisal of ChatGPT-produced text was either "accepted" or "ambivalent" was larger than "rejected" (Table 4).

For example, the results of the first Chi-Square (χ^2) test were significant (χ^2 = 4.804, N=20, p = .028, *Phi* (φ) = .490), indicating that the proportions of correct assignments and incorrect assignments were significantly different between those in which the student's appraisal of definition was "ambivalent" and "rejected." In the 16 correct assignments, the students' appraisal of definition was "ambivalent" in 15 (93.8%), which was higher than the presence of rejections 1 (6.2%). In the four incorrect assignments, the appraisals were 2 (50%) as "ambivalent" and 2 (50%) as "rejected" on the definition.

Sequence three: Learning outcomes by the appraisal of application

In sequence three, the instructor-prompted ChatGPT-produced text was provided at the beginning of instructional task. Results indicated that the proportion of correct assignments in which the students' appraisal of

Table 3. Chi-square comparison tests for definition in sequence 2.

GPT info-quality as identified	Learning outcomes		Chi-square results		
	0[a]	1[b]	χ^2	p	*Phi* (φ)*
	(n=4)	(n=6)			
Rejected	1 (25%)	3 (50%)	0.625	.429	.250
Ambivalent	3 (75%)	3 (50%)			
	(n=17)	(n=4)			
Rejected	1 (5.9%)	3 (75%)	10.032	.002	.691
Accepted	16 (94.1%)	1 (25%)			
	(n=19)	(n=4)			
Ambivalent	3 (40%)	3 (75%)	6.008	.014	.511
Accepted	16 (60%)	1 (25%)			

Notes:
*All the *Phi* (φ) tests had the same significant level of p as in each of the χ^2 tests.
([1b]) Assignments that the academic concepts were correctly formulated.
([0a]) Assignments that the academic concepts were not correctly formulated.

Table 4. Chi-square comparison tests for definition in sequence 3.

GPT info-quality as identified	Learning outcomes		Chi-square results		
	0[a]	1[b]	χ^2	*p*	*Phi (φ)**
	($n=4$)	($n=16$)			
Rejected	2 (50%)	1 (6.2%)	4.804	.028	.490
Ambivalent	2 (50%)	15 (93.8%)			
	($n=2$)	($n=7$)			
Rejected	2 (100%)	1 (14.2%)	5.143	.023	.756
Accepted	0 (0 %)	6 (85.8%)			
	($n=2$)	($n=21$)			
Ambivalent	2 (100%)	15 (71.4%)	0.773	.379	.183
Accepted	0 (0 %)	6 (28.6%)			

Notes:
*All the *Phi (φ)* tests had the same significant level of *p* as in each of the χ^2 tests.
(1[b]) Assignments that the academic concepts were correctly formulated.
(0[a]) Assignments that the academic concepts were not correctly formulated.

Table 5. Chi-square comparison tests for application in sequence 3.

GPT info-quality as identified	Learning outcomes		Chi-square results		
	0[a]	1[b]	χ^2	*p*	*Phi (φ)**
	($n=6$)	($n=9$)			
Rejected	4 (66.7%)	0 (0%)	8.182	.004	.739
Ambivalent	2 (33.3 %)	9 (100%)			
	($n=5$)	($n=11$)			
Rejected	4 (80%)	2 (18.2%)	5.605	.018	.592
Accepted	1 (20 %)	9 (81.8%)			
	($n=1$)	($n=18$)			
Ambivalent	0 (0%)	9 (50%)	0.950	.330	.224
Accepted	1 (100%)	9 (50%)			

Notes:
*All the *Phi (φ)* tests had the same significant level of *p* as in each of the χ^2 tests.
(1[b]) Assignments that the academic concepts were correctly formulated.
(0[a]) Assignments that the academic concepts were not correctly formulated.

ChatGPT-produced text was identified as either "accepted" or "ambivalent" was larger than those which were "rejected" (Table 5).

For example, the results of the second Chi-Square (χ^2) test were significant (χ^2= 5.605, $N=16$, p = .018, Phi (φ) = .592), indicating that the proportions of correct assignments and incorrect assignments were significantly different between those in which the ChatGPT-produced text was appraised as "accepted" and as "rejected." In the 11 correct assignments, nine (81.8%) were appraisals of application were "accepted," which was higher than the two (18.2%) that were appraised as "rejected." The five incorrect assignments included 1 (20%) as "accepted" and four (80%) as "rejected" on the appraisal of application.

Summary of the findings

1. Student appraisal of *definition* in ChatGPT-produced text is associated with expected learning outcomes that the academic concepts were correctly formulated in all three instructional sequences:

a. In sequence one (instructor-prompted), the proportion of correct assignments in which the ChatGPT-produced definition was identified as "accepted" was larger than the proportion identified as "rejected" or "ambivalent."
b. In sequence two (student-prompted), the proportion of correct assignments in which the ChatGPT-produced definition was identified as "accepted" was smaller than the proportion identified as "rejected" or "ambivalent."
c. In sequence three (instructor-prompted), the proportion of correct assignments in which the ChatGPT-produced definition was identified as either "accepted" or "ambivalent" was larger than the proportion identified as "rejected".

2. Student appraisals of *application* in ChatGPT-produced text is associated with expected learning outcomes when the academic concepts were correctly formulated in learning sequence three:

   a. In sequence three (instructor-prompted), the proportion of correct assignments in which the ChatGPT-produced application identified as either "accepted" or "ambivalent" was larger than the proportion identified as "rejected".

Summary of effect size

In Chi-square test, effect size measurements *Phi* φ (for a two-by-two design) and *Cramer's V* when the contingency table is larger than a two-by-two design and are used to quantify the strength of association between two categorical variables. The effect size values of (.1), (.3), and (.5) are considered small, medium and large, respectively (Cohen, 2013). In this study, the *Cramer's V* values ranged from (.620) to (.806) for tests that were significant in research question one, and the *Phi* (φ) values ranged from (.490) to (.756) for Chi-square tests that were significant in research question two, indicating medium to large effect sizes. They were also consistent with the expected effect sizes set in the priori power analysis, ranged from (.50) to (.65), determining the range of the sample size for this study.

The effect sizes in relevant studies were reviewed. Sehlaoui and Shinge (2013) conducted chi-square tests to examine the knowledge in applied linguistics for English language teachers and the effect size *Phi* (φ) values ranged from .243 to .301 (N=201). Payaprom and Payaprom (2020) examined language learners' learning style by majors, and the *Cramer's V*was .15 (N=372). Another study on teacher education investigating the extent to which learning style associated with gender and type of education (Can,

2009) revealed the calculated*Cramer's V* values of .20 and .21 (Ben et al., 2023). Compared with relevant studies in the literature, effect sizes in this study were relatively larger than those from the literature.

Discussion and conclusion

Set within Vygotsky's (1986) sociocultural framework, this study builds upon on previous research confirming the potential of ChatGPT-produced text to enhance preservice teachers' understanding of pedagogical content toward the use of academic concepts (Case & Liu, 2024, under review). The content analysis suggests that the students recognized the potential of ChatGPT to produce accurate and even useful definitions but doubted its ability to produce instruction (application) responsive to the cultural and linguistic needs of multilingual students. In their appraisals of ChatGPT-produced texts, they emphasized the importance of the human element in instruction and questioned whether or not ChatGPT was capable of producing instruction without a teacher's guidance. How the findings reflect the tension between definition and their thoughts about the importance of the human element in instruction (application) is explored below.

Before a discussion of the findings, it is necessary to address the limitations of this exploratory study. First, the study employed a nonrandomized within-subject design, using two sections of an existing class with a relatively small sample size ($N = 30$). The results and findings are not generalizable to larger populations. Second, three instructional sequences and three learning tasks were examined in this study. The ChatGPT-produced texts including definition, application, and technical concerns were based on particular prompts related only to these instructional sequences. The interpretation of the results and findings was limited to the context of this exploratory study. Drawing on firsthand experiences of preservice teachers, this exploratory study suggests practical means of ChatGPT-integrated learning for further exploration. Further studies would benefit from empirical design with a larger random sample, and with a variety of means of ChatGPT integrated methods, procedures, sequences, learning conditions and learning tasks.

Overall appraisal of ChatGPT-produced text

With respect to research question one, findings suggest that the overall appraisal of definition was associated with students' correct use of the academic concept across all three sequences. In the instructor-prompted instructional sequences one and three, among preservice teachers who achieved an academic concept in their assignment, findings reveal a higher proportion of students either accepted or were ambivalent toward the use of ChatGPT-produced definition (Tables 2 and 4). Ambivalent appraisals, again across all sequences, typically balanced praise for its rhetorical and organizational skills with questions about its inherent inability to factor emotion, culture, and human experience into its explanations. An example from sequence one captures the sentiment.

> With regards to [its effectiveness], I think ChatGPT was able to create a coherent essay that answered the prompt. However, I also believe that there was a lack of serious analysis, reflecting a lack of ability to understand the relationship between language and culture, since this is an experience that is extremely human in nature. Although it is able to think in language in the same way we do, it cannot apply that language in the same way, because of the fact that it does not have a human experience.

The student's praise for 'coherent' writing in ChatGPT-produced text is supported by Katz et al. (2023) and Gilson et al. (2022), but her ambivalence also suggests a growing awareness that education is a human enterprise. She argues that "serious analysis" of the linguistic and cultural issues that fuel an understanding of the instruction of multilingual learners excludes ChatGPT-produced text. Throughout the remaining assignments, students would use ChatGPT-produced text as the straw dummy in the debate over whether or not human experience is prerequisite to understanding the instruction of multilingual students.

Further exploration of appraisals in ChatGPT-produced text

With respect to research question two, findings from sequence three suggest at least two important points. First, careful preparation and strategic use of ChatGPT-produced content can widen students' appraisals of ChatGPT-produced content of both definition and application. Specifically, placing ChatGPT-produced text that is teacher-prompted at the beginning of the instructional task can inspire appraisal of both definition and application, which, potentially, could lead to a broad understanding of the academic concept. The association between the correct use of the academic concept and appraisal of both definition (χ^2= 10.887, p = .012) and application (χ^2 = 17.532, p < .001) was significant only in sequence three.

Second, findings from sequence three instigated research question two, a deeper examination of the students' appraisals from the three sequences. Findings revealed that among students who reached an academic concept in their writing, a significantly higher proportion either accepted use of ChatGPT, (81.8%), compared with those who rejected (18.2%), or were ambivalent about its use. In the instructor-prompted instructional sequences one and three, among students who achieved an academic concept in their assignment, findings revealed a higher proportion of students who had either accepted or were ambivalent to use ChatGPT-produced definition

(Tables 2 and 4). However, in sequence two, students who did not reach an academic concept either accepted (94.1%) or were ambivalent (75%) to use the ChatGPT-produced definition. In contrast, those who achieved the academic concepts identified a lower proportion for accepted (25%) and ambivalent (50%).

One explanation for the wider variation found in sequence two might be that it is the only student-prompted sequence. Students may be entering prompts of varying quality into ChatGPT, resulting in ChatGPT-produced texts of varying quality that may or may not be relevant to the correct academic concept. This is consistent with research on the influence of prompts on the quality of ChatGPT-produced texts. Gilson et al. (2022), for instance, noted that ChatGPT is not able to interpret tables or figures and provides higher quality responses when given sample questions. The data did not show evidence that the preservice teachers were aware of this. While some discovered that it took multiple prompts to receive a satisfactory response from ChatGPT, there was no evidence of them questioning the responses because of ChatGPT's inability to interpret tables of figures.

In conclusion, ChatGPT-produced texts provide a valuable resource in LTE, but its use requires the guiding hand of the teacher educator. As such, learning with ChatGPT-produced text begins with teacher-prompted instruction and attention to its placement within the instructional sequence. As the more knowledgeable other, the teacher educator is best equipped to assess the extent to which ChatGPT articulates an understanding of the selected academic concept and employ the use of ChatGPT-produced text to open discussions which expand students' thinking about the human element in instruction.

Implications for practice

The findings suggest a place for the use of ChatGPT within a sociocultural framework and the need to consider how ChatGPT can be used in a socially and culturally mediated environment. Vygotsky's (1986) theory demonstrates that learning is a socially-situated experience in which cultural tools, which include language and technology, enhance cognitive development. For the teacher educator, the introduction of ChatGPT presents new opportunities to create structured mediated spaces which challenge preservice teachers to advance their understanding of pedagogical content toward an academic concept. Throughout the process, preservice teachers come to see ChatGPT as a valuable tool which mediates their learning but also requires them to actively critique its content. Exploring the tension between these two roles provides a powerful forum for preservice teachers to examine their own emerging understanding of pedagogy, ultimately preparing them to integrate AI-driven technology into their own instruction.

Teacher educators can begin with prompting preservice teachers to examine their own their current perceptions of ChatGPT. Attitudes about ChatGPT are predictive of the frequency and ways that preservice teachers use ChatGPT in the classroom (Javier & Moorhouse, 2024; Moorhouse, 2024; Moorhouse & Kohnke, 2024; Yang & Appleget, 2024). Because many may not have extensive experience with ChatGPT (Moorhouse, 2024), opportunities to read about its potential to create lessons and classroom exercises (e.g., Farrokhnia et al., 2024; Skrabut, 2023) can be valuable. Teacher educators can prompt preservice teachers to reflect on its potential in the classroom in class discussions. The experience provides what Johnson and Golombek (2020) refer to as a play/stepping into teaching, as it provides a space for preservice teachers to try out new ideas in a safe space under the guidance of a more knowledgeable other.

Next, teacher educators can problematize the content and use of ChatGPT by asking them to explore the interplay between technology and human experience. This might be done in a number of ways. Examples from this study included critiquing ChatGPT-created lessons and essays, asking preservice teachers to compare ChatGPT-produced essays on pedagogical topics with their own writing and responding to ChatGPT-produced posts in discussion boards. Next, teacher educators can press students to work independently with ChatGPT to create lessons and pedagogical content while still providing guidance as the knowledgeable other. Finally, more research is needed on the ways in which ChatGPT can provide a forum for how teaching is a human-centered occupation.

These findings are a call for research on the nature and potential use of ChatGPT-produced texts in the teacher education classroom. This study spoke to the importance of teacher-guided experiences when introducing ChatGPT-produced texts, but the preservice teachers in this study were enrolled in their first and only class on teaching multilingual learners. This opens questions for future research on preservice teachers who are more knowledgeable of pedagogical content and LTE. Do they require the same level of scaffolding when using ChatGPT-produced texts? If so, how should that scaffolding proceed? Finally, this study also raised questions about the extent to which ChatGPT is able produce text which is reflective of multilingual students' culture and learning experiences. Students identified this as the human element, and it is important divide that has to be better understood as teacher educators move forward within integrating AI-based texts and materials into their classrooms. Researchers might continue to explore the ways that ChatGPT-produced lessons can inspire discussions and learning on the importance of the human element in instruction but there are many more avenues which could both incorporate preservice teachers' experiences in K-12 classrooms and teacher education courses.

The introduction of ChatGPT in 2022 and subsequent research in teacher education regarding its classroom possibilities represent a clarion call for teacher educators to engage in a dialogue on its use. Framed within a sociocultural framework, the use of ChatGPT-produced text in LTE should be leveraged to advance preservice students toward a deeper understanding of pedagogical content. More broadly, this study encourages a curriculum and instructional practices which encourage preservice teachers to confront how language, culture and human experience shape the instruction of multilingual students. Achieving this will push teacher educators to integrate ChatGPT in ways that go beyond the polemics of "ChatGPT versus human instruction," fostering a deeper discussion about the interconnection of language, culture, and human experience.

Disclosure statement

No potential conflict of interest was reported by the author(s).

ORCID

Rod Case http://orcid.org/0000-0003-1175-648X
Leping Liu http://orcid.org/0000-0001-5859-8189

References

Case, R., & Liu, L. (2024). ChatGPT in language teacher education: Bridging everyday concepts and academic concepts through a sociocultural lens. Submitted to *The New Educator* for publication, under review.

Ben, Shachar, M. S., Patil, I., Thériault, R., Wiernik, B. M., & Lüdecke, D. (2023). Phi, Fei, Fo, Fum: Effect sizes for categorical data that use the chi-squared statistic. *Mathematics*, *11*(9), 1982. 2023, https://doi.org/10.3390/math11091982

Can, S. (2009). The effects of science student teachers' academic achievements, their grade levels, gender and type of education they are exposed to on their 4mat learning styles. *Procedia - Social and Behavioral Sciences*, *1*(1), 1853–1857. https://doi.org/10.1016/j.sbspro.2009.01.327

Ciechanowski, L., Przegalinska, A., Magnuski, M., & Gloor, P. (2019). In the shades of the uncanny valley: An experimental study of human–chatbot interaction. *Future Generation Computer Systems*, *92*, 539–548. https://doi.org/10.1016/j.future.2018.01.055

Cohen, J. (1960). A coefficient of agreement for nominal scales. *Educational and Psychological Measurement*, *20*(1), 37–46. https://doi.org/10.1177/001316446002000104

Cohen, J. (2013). Statistical power analysis for the behavioral sciences Routledge. https://doi.org/10.4324/9780203771587

Cooper, G. (2023). Examining science education in CHATGPT: An exploratory study of Generative Artificial Intelligence. *Journal of Science Education and Technology*, *32*(3), 444–452. https://doi.org/10.1007/s10956-023-10039-y

de Souza, M. (2017). Understanding Mexican immigrant students in American schools: A case study of two *preparatorias* in México. *Cogent Education*, *4*(1), 1387963. https://doi.org/10.1080/2331186X.2017.1387963

Elkins, K., & Chun, J. (2020). Can GPT-3 pass a writer's Turing test? *Journal of Cultural Analytics*, *5*(2). https://doi.org/10.22148/001c.17212

Farrokhnia, M., Banihashem, S. K., Noroozi, O., & Wals, A. (2024). A SWOT analysis of CHATGPT: Implications for educational practice and Research. *Innovations in Education and Teaching International*, *61*(3), 460–474. https://doi.org/10.1080/14703297.2023.2195846

Gilson, A., Safranek, C., Huang, T., Socrates, V., Chi, L., Taylor, R. A., & Chartash, D. (2022). *How does ChatGPT perform on the medical licensing exams? The implications of large language models for medical education and knowledge assessment.* https://doi.org/10.1101/2022.12.23.22283901

Goldsmith, J. S., & Kurpius, S. E. (2018). Fostering the academic success of their children: Voices of Mexican immigrant parents. *The Journal of Educational Research*, *111*(5), 564–573. https://doi.org/10.1080/00220671.2017.1323717

Hanselman, K., & Liu, L. (2021). Characteristics of initial posts and peer engagement: Density score analyses for social presence in online discussions. *Journal of Educational Technology Development and Exchange*, *14*(2), 41–74. https://doi.org/10.18785/jetde.1402.03

Huh, S. (2023). Are ChatGPT's knowledge and interpretation ability comparable to those of medical students in Korea for taking a parasitology examination? A descriptive study. *Journal of Educational Evaluation for Health Professions*, *20*, 1. https://doi.org/10.3352/jeehp.2023.20.1

Javier, D. R., & Moorhouse, B. L. (2024). Developing secondary school English language learners' productive and critical use of ChatGPT. *TESOL Journal*, *15*(2). https://doi.org/10.1002/tesj.755

Jeon, J., & Lee, S. (2023). Large language models in education: A focus on the complementary relationship between human teachers and ChatGPT. *Education and Information Technologies*, *28*(12), 15873–15892. https://doi.org/10.1007/s10639-023-11834-1

Johnson, K. E., & Golombek, P. R. (2020). Informing and transforming language teacher education pedagogy. *Language Teaching Research*, *24*(1), 116–127. https://doi.org/10.1177/1362168818777539

Katz, D. M., Bommarito, M. J., Gao, S., & Arredondo, P. (2023). GPT-4 passes the bar exam. *SSRN Electronic Journal*. https://doi.org/10.2139/ssrn.4389233

Khalaf, M. A. (2024). Does attitude towards plagiarism predict Aigiarism using ChatGPT? *AI and Ethics*. https://doi.org/10.1007/s43681-024-00426-5

Kohnke, L., Moorhouse, B. L., & Zou, D. (2023). ChatGPT for language teaching and learning. *RELC Journal*, *54*(2), 537–550. https://doi.org/10.1177/00336882231162868

Kostka, I., & Toncelli, R, Northeastern University (2023). Exploring applications of ChatGPT to English language teaching: Opportunities, challenges, and recommendations. *Teaching English as a Second or Foreign Language-TESL-EJ*, *27*(3). https://doi.org/10.55593/ej.27107int

Landis, J. R., & Koch, G. G. (1977). The measurement of observer agreement for categorical data. *Biometrics*, *33*(1), 159–174. https://doi.org/10.1080/10543406.2016.1273941

Lantolf, J. P., Xi, J., & Minakova, V. (2021). Sociocultural theory and concept-based language instruction. *Language Teaching*, *54*(3), 327–342. https://doi.org/10.1017/S0261444820000348

Li, T., Ji, Y., & Zhan, Z. (2024). Expert or machine? comparing the effect of pairing student teacher with in-service teacher and CHATGPT on their critical thinking, learning performance, and cognitive load in an integrated-stem course. *Asia Pacific Journal of Education*, *44*(1), 45–60. https://doi.org/10.1080/02188791.2024.2305163

Liu, L. (2023). Analyzing the text content produced by ChatGPT: Prompts, feature-components in responses, and a predictive model. *Journal of Educational Technology Development and Exchange*, *16*(1), 49–70. https://doi.org/10.18785/jetde.1601.03

Moll, L. C. (2019). Elaborating funds of knowledge: Community-oriented practices in international contexts. *Literacy Research: Theory, Method, and Practice*, *68*(1), 130–138. https://doi.org/10.1177/2381336919870805

Moorhouse, B. L. (2024). Beginning and first-year language teachers' readiness for the generative AI age. *Computers and Education: Artificial Intelligence*, *6*, 100201. https://doi.org/10.1016/j.caeai.2024.100201

Moorhouse, B. L., & Kohnke, L. (2024). The effects of generative AI on initial language teacher education: The perceptions of teacher educators. *System*, *122*, 103290. https://doi.org/10.1016/j.system.2024.103290

Nicolaidou, I., Pissas, P., & Boglou, D. (2023). Comparing immersive Virtual Reality to mobile applications in foreign language learning in higher education: A quasi-experiment. *Interactive Learning Environments*, *31*(4), 2001–2015. https://doi.org/10.1080/10494820.2020.1870504

Payaprom, S., & Payaprom, Y. (2020). Identifying learning styles of language learners: A useful step in moving towards the learner-centred approach. *Journal of Language and Linguistic Studies*, *16*(1), 59–72. https://doi.org/10.17263/jlls.712646

Rourke, L., Anderson, T., Garrison, D. R., & Archer, W. (2001). Assessing social presence in asynchronous, text-based computer conferencing. *Journal of Distance Education*, *14*(3), 51–70. Retrieved October10, 2024 from https://www.ijede.ca/index.php/jde/article/view/153

Rusandi, M Arli, Saripah, Ipah, Khairun, Deasy Yunika, Ahman, Mutmainnah, (2023). No worries with CHATGPT: Building bridges between artificial intelligence and education with critical thinking soft skills. *Journal of Public Health (Oxford, England)*, *45*(3, e602–e603). https://doi.org/10.1093/pubmed/fdad049

Sehlaoui, A. S., & Shinge, M. (2013). The pursuit of quality over quantity in TESOL teacher education: Coursework Versus test only. *TESOL Journal*, *4*(1), 106–128. https://doi.org/10.1002/tesj.53

Shabani, K. (2016). Applications of Vygotsky's sociocultural approach for teachers' professional development. *Cogent Education*, *3*(1), 1252177. https://doi.org/10.1080/2331186X.2016.1252177

Skrabut, S. (2023). *80 ways to use ChatGPT in the classroom: Using AI to enhance teaching and learning*. Sandman Books.

Solorza, C., Aponte, g., Leverenz, T., Becker, T., & Frias, B. (2023). (rep.). Translanguaging in dual language bilingual education: A blueprint for planning units of study (pp. 8–88). CUNY-NYSIEB, The Graduate Center, The City University of New York.

van den Berg, G., & Du Plessis, E. (2023). CHATGPT and Generative AI: Possibilities for its contribution to lesson planning, critical thinking and openness in teacher education. *Education Sciences*, *13*(10), 998. https://doi.org/10.3390/educsci13100998

Vygotsky, L. S. (1986). *Thought and language*. Translated by A. Kozulin MIT Press.

Weber, R. P. (1990). *Basic content analysis* Sage Publications.

Williamson, M. (2024). Sample size calculation with GPower. Retrieved June 20, 2024 from: https://med.und.edu/research/daccota/_files/pdfs/berdc_resource_pdfs/sample_size_gpower_module.pdf

Yang, S., & Appleget, C. (2024). An exploration of preservice teachers' perceptions of generative AI: Applying the technological acceptance model. *Journal of Digital Learning in Teacher Education*, *40*(3), 159–172. https://doi.org/10.1080/21532974.2024.2367573

Yeadon, W., Inyang, O.-O., Mizouri, A., Peach, A., & Testrow, C. P. (2023). The death of the short-form physics essay in the Coming AI Revolution. *Physics Education*, *58*(3), 035027. https://doi.org/10.1088/1361-6552/acc5cf

Zhai, X. (2022). CHATGPT user experience: Implications for education. *SSRN Electronic Journal*. https://doi.org/10.2139/ssrn.4312418

Zwiers, J. (2014). *Building academic language: Meeting common core standards across disciplines, grades 5–12*. Jossey-Bass.

Index

Note: **Bold** page numbers refer to tables and *italic* page numbers refer to figures.